Building a Foundation *for* Suffering

Biblical Truths to Thrive in Chaotic Times

William S. Cain, DMin

Foreword by Michael A. Milton, PhD

Building a Foundation for Suffering

Trilogy Christian Publishers

A Wholly Owned Subsidary of Trinity Broadcasting Network

2442 Michelle Drive

Tustin, CA 92780

For information, address Trilogy Christian Publishing Rights Department, 2442 Michelle Drive, Tustin, CA 92780.

Trilogy Christian Publishing/ TBN and colophon are trademarks of Trinity Broadcasting Network.

For information about special discounts for bulk purchases, please contact Trilogy Christian Publishing.

10 9 8 7 6 5 4 3 2 1

Library of Congress Cataloging-in-Publication Data is available.

ISBN: 979-8-89333-503-3

ISBN: 979-8-89333-504-0

Endorsements

"Suffering will change you!" These are the words of my good friend, Dr. Bill Cain. I remember talking with him about plans for his dissertation. Bill was frustrated. In spite of all the work he had poured into his study of the Book of Job, he was not able to gain the traction he needed to begin writing. Several months passed, and we returned to our previous conversation. But this time, things went in a different direction. We were in the midst of the COVID-19 Pandemic, and sickness and death were seemingly everywhere. It was at this point that Bill realized he was no longer dealing with suffering in the abstract but in the harsh concrete reality that was changing the face of North America. Long the land of abundant doctors and nurses and unsurpassed medical care, the world had changed, and suddenly, the biblical teachings on suffering were relevant in a new way. Working with a small group, Bill was building a foundation for suffering! I cannot tell you how pleased I am that this series of teachings, borne in the reality of suffering and death, is available to ministers and other caregivers to remind us that God is with us in our suffering and will use it to make us look more like Jesus.

— **R. J. Gore Jr., D.Min., Ph.D.**
Professor of Systematic Theology and Dean Emeritus
Erskine Theological Seminary

This is a wonderful book. My former student, Bill Cain, once a keen business leader, now a pastor, has looked into suffering's face from a number of perspectives, including personal experience. He writes with a pastor's heart and with insight, integrity, and clarity and offers practical biblical counsel. Read what Bill writes. You will be better for it.

— **Robert Leslie Holmes, D.Min., Ph.D**.
Retired seminary Provost and fifty-year-plus pastor

This book contains a theology of suffering that is much needed in today's Christian Church. I found it comforting, convicting, and extraordinarily helpful as I seek to pastor God's people through the trials and troubles of life. Most of all, I was encouraged in my own walk with Christ and that my Savior is all-sufficient for any suffering that I may face. This book is a helpful read and will also be a helpful resource for future ministry.

— **Rev. Matthew H. Kuiken,**
Senior Minister, First ARP Church of Gastonia, NC.

In a society that constantly offers us medicines, natural supplements, seminars, and luxury cruises in an effort to tell us that all discomfort in life is undesirable, Dr. Bill Cain approaches suffering head-on. By looking carefully at Scripture, he shows us that suffering for the believer is normal, can be fully embraced by trusting in the goodness of God, and can even be an occasion of rejoicing.

— Dr. Loyd Melton,
Distinguished Professor of New Testament Emeritus
Erskine Theological Seminary

Foreword

It may well be the single greatest intellectual and existential obstacle to Christianity: "How can a good God allow"—and you know the rest. The painful reality of human suffering co-existing with the doctrine of the sovereignty of God remains an enigma that must be faced by both unbelievers and believers in the Lord Jesus. Indeed, each generation needs a fresh voice to speak God's revealed truth to this perennial question. Our times, described as a "Secular Age" by Charles Taylor, are marked not only by the loss of a coherent story that provides meaning to life but also by the epistemology to form questions. Consequently, many of our friends and neighbors are drifting farther away from the immovable *terra firma* of biblical revelation that shapes reason and brings hope. The farther we drift from the shore of the Judeo-Christian worldview, the more dangerous things become. The vicissitudes of life can become a veritable riptide of mystery, a black hole of despair that devours. It is, therefore, not compassionate to remain quiet or passive as we witness such suffering without meaning, despair without hope, and anguish without end.

Throughout the centuries, some of the most beloved

figures have been those who offer a cogent and faithful response to such desperate scenes of suffering. Their presence through teaching truth is not only a calming presence in the storm but a lifeline in catastrophe. Thus, we seek wisdom in our dark nights and help in our grief from authors like Saint John of the Cross and C. S. Lewis (and we are not ashamed to add the voices of Calvin and Luther, whose theological assertions admitted sovereignty and suffering along with mystery by bringing theodicy to the cross of Christ, depositing the great philosophical questions of life at the very holy ground where revelation and secret counsel meet).

Yet, we say again: we need not only faithful voices from history's marbled halls but wise Christian shepherds for today: contextual, accessible, relatable. And that leads us to the book you are about to read, the experience you are embarking upon, and the shepherd who will guide you.

I am sure you will agree with me that the Reverend Dr. William "Bill" Cain is that shepherd. Dr. Cain's scholarly yet remarkably pastoral voice must now be counted among that exclusive company of Christian voices who have addressed the question of suffering and the Christian life. William Cain does so with insight born of faith, wisdom shaped by life and ministry, and scholarship proven by considerable mentors.

I am thus most honored to commend the new book by my fellow Tarheel (and Erskine Seminary) alumnus Rev. Dr. William (Bill) Cain. Dr. Cain has produced a remarkable work on human suffering that is distinguished by faithful exegesis and exposition of the biblical testimony, insightful interaction with the relevant literature, and—this is key—a Christ-like teaching that is deeply personal and thereby helpfully accessible. Taken together, these qualities become a rare and precious gift to those within and outside of the Church. We need what Dr. Cain writes now more than ever. I am thankful to commend this book on suffering by Bill Cain with the prayer that many will read it and come to know the spiritual healing that is made available from its pages.

—Michael A. Milton, PhD

President and Senior Fellow, Faith for Living, Inc., and The D. James Kennedy Institute of Reformed Leadership; Chaplain (Colonel), US Army (Ret.); CEO/Chancellor (Ret.), Reformed Theological Seminary; Distinguished Professor of Missions and Evangelism, Erskine Theological Seminary; Board-certified Pastoral Counselor Pentecost Sunday, 2024

DEDICATION

My ministry to those in pain, trauma, and chaos has been shaped by my journey through suffering individually and with those I have tried to counsel and shepherd in the name of Jesus Christ. Therefore, my dissertation is dedicated to all those who have graciously ministered to me in my times of need.

In particular, I dedicate this work to two people. First, to the little girl from Gaston Christian School who, so long ago, traced her hand on a piece of paper and wrote there so that I could place my hand on top of her traced hand and would never feel alone. Thank you for that constant reminder of the love of God and the love of community. Second and most of all, to Dr. Daniel Patton, friend, mentor, advisor, and brother in the Lord. Your work on this project was beneficial, but far more importantly, you have modeled for me what it means to suffer in the name of Jesus Christ. To God be the Glory.

TABLE OF CONTENTS

Preface

My great-grandfather and his brother bought Page Lumber Co. in 1910 and renamed it Spencer Lumber Company in the Gastonia, North Carolina area. In the 1920s, my grandfather, William Theodore (W. T.) Spencer, for whom I am named, joined them. My father and uncle both worked there, and my first job at age six was there each Saturday, sweeping the floors and emptying the trash. For my efforts, I was paid one dollar, which I promptly spent in the hardware section of the sprawling complex for a tool I did not yet own. I remember the lumber yard and the shop complex, where they made their doors, windows, and moldings. I grew up loving to work with wood and nails. My father taught me to bury a silver dollar under the foundation of every house so the owner would never go broke!

My childhood love for building things may be why I love the story of Jesus's teaching in Luke, where he talks about what those who follow him are like. He says, "He is like a man building a house, who dug down deep and laid the foundation on rock. When a flood came, the torrent struck that house but could not shake it, because it had been well built" (Luke 6:48-49, NIV). A strong foundation built on the rock is critical to every structure.

The text indicates that a flood will come eventually. Suffering in life is like that as well. It will come to everyone at some point. The story says the one who built a house without a strong foundation immediately lost it when the storm came. So, it is with our faith. Suffering will come into every life at some point. What we build our faith on will determine if our faith will survive the storms of life. The importance of our foundation is critical to thriving in the chaos of life. This book grew out of my suffering from cancer, family deaths, and my struggles. I pray that the foundation stones mentioned here will help you build a solid foundation for your faith, built on the rock of our gracious God. Almost fifty times in Scripture, God or Jesus is referred to as the rock.

These doctrinal truths are found all over the Bible. From one garden in Eden to the one in the New Jerusalem, Scripture is full of what we need to build our faith for suffering. These six foundational truths are not all-inclusive; more could have been written about each one. But I hope the information here will lead you to dig deeper into each one.

I have tried to footnote where appropriate. However, I have read and studied this topic for over twenty-five years, and I am sure I have missed noting an original source that has become just part of my mindset on suffering. Please do not hesitate to correct me. I welcome your input. Many authors, mentors, and friends have assisted me in this effort, but I ultimately offer this to you for God's Kingdom. To God be the Glory!

ACKNOWLEDGMENTS

Above all else, I praise and thank God for the opportunity to pursue this degree and the chance to write this book. As a pastor, I have experienced and seen much suffering. Suffering never leaves you the same, so my ministry has evolved by God's grace.

I am so thankful for my wife, Monica, who endured my sickness with me and has never wavered in our calling to ministry. I also thank her for being my editorial support at each step of my academic and ministerial life. She has carried the load as I worked.

I thank my dear friend, Dr. Daniel Patton, for his insights, suggestions, and support in completing this work. I also thank Cheryl Sanford for her valuable input and editing.

I thank my mentor and friend, Dr. R. J. Gore, for his persistent love, support, instruction, wisdom, and calming voice. I would not have completed this degree without his unending encouragement. I also thank Dr. Loyd Melton for his support and help all along the way and Dr. George Schwab for his work with me in my study of the Book of Job.

I appreciate the elders in my church, Louisville Associate Reformed Presbyterian Church, for allowing me the time and space to complete this effort. I have felt their support at every turn. I also acknowledge my congregation, which has allowed me to love them through their times of suffering.

CHAPTER ONE

BUILDING A FOUNDATION
FOR SUFFERING

September 2001 was not only a month that will live in the collective minds of all Americans alive on the eleventh day of the month, but it was also a month in which I had surgery on my neck. My dear friend and prayer partner, Dr. Kevin Weiss, walked into the recovery room after surgery to tell me and my wife that the surgery was "boringly routine." I had noticed a lump in the side of my neck several weeks earlier. After consultation with my doctor, he told me that he thought it was simply a stopped-up parotid salivary gland. Men my age sometimes get them. While it was an involved surgery requiring more than a twelve-inch incision from above my ear to the base of my neck, he would simply remove the gland. The surgery results usually included the nerves growing back at cross purposes so that my mouth would water when I should be sweating, and my face would sweat when my mouth should salivate before a great meal.

As we sat in Kevin's office for a follow-up appointment, he seemed delayed, taking longer than usual to come into the room. Finally, he came into the small white room, and we saw on his face an expression that immediately caused my heart to race. His words to me this time were different. He said, "Bill, I don't know how to tell you this, but you have cancer." Many others have heard these words as well. Everyone who has heard them knows that life pivots into chaos at that moment.

That dreaded word I heard was a complete surprise. I was too young for cancer at forty-one. I had a wonderful wife and three small children. I had a company to run and ministry work to do. Cancer was for older folks. Although I had never smoked, I had cancer in my neck. To add to the turmoil, the type of cancer I had was so rare that there was little information available on what to do next, how to treat it, or even a long-term prognosis. What followed was weeks of appointments with doctors, second opinions, and meetings with an oncologist and radiologist. Chemotherapy and radiation treatments followed. Time marched on, but life seemed to be put on hold. Pain, suffering, fear, anxiety, and chaos all seemed to fight for first place in my emotions. How could God allow me to suffer so? I was teaching and serving in my church as an elder. I was busy for Jesus. Yet, my call that year was to learn to suffer in Christ.

I cried, wept with my wife, and tried to be strong for my kids. My church prayed for me and over me. I had the privilege of being the board chairperson at Gaston Christian School in Gastonia, North Carolina. The children would send me cards of encouragement, one drawing a hand on her card. As I opened it, the little girl had written around the trace of her hand, "If you are lonely, place your hand over mine, and I am with you." The community was so supportive, and yet, I felt like God was not hearing my prayers. Why me? How could I die and leave Monica with three small children?

By God's grace, I have been cancer-free for over twenty-two years. My face still droops a bit from all the surgery and treatment, and my mouth is still very dry from having all my salivary glands burned out in radiation. My taste has changed, and my neck is weak and hurts much of the time because of missing or weakened muscles. However, God carried me every day of my suffering.

What I learned during those months of suffering, not being able to eat or drink and feeding myself only through a tube, was that I did not have a full biblical foundation to handle my suffering. My theodicy was underdeveloped, and my theology of suffering was incomplete. My faith was in Christ as Lord and Savior, but I was not prepared to understand my suffering and how not to waste it. While I had faith in God, I had not processed a full understanding of suffering. I realized that the confidence I had was not fully based in Christ but more on my own self-confidence. Suffering has a strange way of stripping us of our pride, arrogance, and self-sufficiency. We realize we are not in control of our own lives.[1] But out of this test of fire, my heart grew to desire to understand suffering more fully and to walk with others as they suffered.

The psalmist wrote in Psalm 11:3, "When the foundations are being destroyed, what can the righteous do?"[2] Pain and suffering have been a part of life since the fall of mankind. When Adam and Eve sinned, pain and suffering entered all of creation in both nature and humanity (Genesis 3:1-19). As a pastor of a congregation now, I am called to shepherd my congregants and, at times, my community through the valley of chaos and crisis in a way that correctly reflects the character of God and meets people where they are existentially in their time of suffering (1 Peter 5:2-4). This need has only grown exponentially under the burden of the COVID-19 pandemic.

COVID-19 has brought suffering to the Western

world that it has not known since perhaps the plagues of Europe in the sixteenth and seventeenth centuries and certainly not in the United States. While suffering is an issue that everyone deals with in their lives, few Christians have lived through such a prolonged period of suffering in the culture at large with the perfect storm of economic collapse, sickness, death, mental illness because of institutional mandates, and healthcare shortages. Historically, the modern Western world has used technology, medicine, money, and power to minimize and lessen suffering on every front. As a result, the church in America has depended less on God and more on culture and governmental means to support them and carry them in times of difficulty. It would not be too strong a statement to say that the Western church knows little of real suffering as part of a daily way of life or true dependence on a grace-giving God for "our daily bread," especially compared to the church in other regions of the world.

This type of Christian living requires a proper understanding of evil in the world, a strong, biblical theology of suffering, and helpful skills to meet the needs of people in everyday life. Experience teaches that people do not learn such deep doctrinal truths in the middle of pain and suffering. The hope of this work is to teach believers the necessary foundation stones of truth to help them understand suffering from a biblical worldview so that they are comforted in their time of need. Foundations must be built when the winds of life are calm.[3]

As already stated, I have suffered through cancer. I have also suffered the death of my best friend while he ran on the beach when we were in college, a horrific car wreck that almost cost my son the use of his arms and his life, and a niece born with a defective heart. In the third week of my pastorate here in Louisville, Georgia, one of my members, who was a husband and father of two children, committed suicide before I could meet his family. Within six more weeks, one of my deacons called me in tears, screaming that his daughter had been killed in an automobile accident while on the way to her grandmother's funeral.

I have shepherded and cared for a congregation through the pandemic. Suffering surrounds us all. So many people ask the question, "Why?" How do Christians reconcile it all with a loving God? John Stott has written that the problem of pain and suffering is the greatest challenge to the Christian faith when it appears to be so random and out of line with God's love and justice.[4] But suffering is not just an intellectual problem. Indeed, it is also, perhaps most importantly for many, intensely personal. It is never just out there; it is right where we live. At some point, everyone will experience suffering in their lives. During such times, the sufferer is tempted to doubt the goodness of God and his care. How can God be all good and all-powerful, yet this crisis has happened to me? We realize that the theoretical and superficial beliefs we learned in Sunday School do not support us in times when evil and suffering make their home in our lives. Suffering is spiritual warfare with our hearts and minds. It exposes the false gods of our daily lives. Christians who want to endure times of suffering well will have to give serious thought as to how to apply the doctrines of their faith in these chaotic times. As Paul David Tripp writes, God does care and does enter our suffering with us. The Bible is full of hope that is both immediate and eternal.[5]

Suffering will change you. Your foundation in such times will, in large part, determine how you live with and through these difficulties. Your perspective will change. You will view others around you in new ways. What you appreciate may change as well. There is no one shape that fits all in suffering. Equally, we all process chaotic times in unique ways. It is always personal. What often adds to our dilemma is that the wicked seem to prosper in this life, and the righteous seem to suffer the most (Jeremiah 12:1; Job 21:7-14). How can we put all of our experiences and emotions together to make sense? Agnostic-turned-Christian Sheldon Vanauken says that bringing God into the situation in times of pain and suffering can simply be intellectual words that really don't help.[6] The question this book seeks to answer is how God helps us in our times of trouble.

C. S. Lewis wrote what so many believers often feel and observe when he stated that we can feel welcome by God in times of praise when we have no sense of needing Him. But when we come to Him in our time of need, we often feel the door is shut and locked.[7] It is true that many of the Psalms speak to the anger and frustration that believers feel in their time of suffering (Psalm 13:1-6, 35:17-18). Elie Wiesel narrates his journey through a concentration camp in Germany and how he rebelled against God in his suffering. He could not imagine a God who would allow such suffering and pain.[8] His cry is like so many others in the middle of suffering. The other views of God and evil never hold up under careful consideration. It is only the God of the Bible that helps us to make sense of all these questions.

Atheism cannot help the person who is in a time of need. If pain and suffering are just the bad luck we have drawn from evolution, where is there any hope? If God is not all-powerful, then He is powerless to stop evil.[9] The Deist view of God offers no hope because, as the watchmaker of creation, God simply lets history play out without taking any notice. There is no comfort in an absent God. We must hold to a God who is both transcendent and personal because only then can true hope come to those in need. We must recognize that God is all-powerful, all good, and that evil exists in this world.

God stands behind good and evil asymmetrically. All good flows from Him, and evil is never outside His boundaries. He could have created a very different world. God could have created a world in which humanity is simply robotic in our actions. We would only do His will as He programmed us to do. He could have created an amoral world with no sense of good and evil. But the reality is that God created a world in which we have the capacity to love. With that capacity came the ability to sin.[10]

What is man's role in all this trouble? If God is all good and all-powerful and evil exists, the next question I usually get is, "Isn't God responsible for my suffering?" How do human free will and God's sovereignty come together? The Bible holds in tension that man is fully responsible for his own sin and God sovereignly controls whatsoever comes to pass (Genesis 48; Acts 2:23). It is completely God's sovereignty and completely man's own will to sin.[11]

In this world, Christians will suffer in a variety of ways. The sinfulness of our hearts and the fallenness of the world we live in bring us pain, sorrow, and struggles. These are the results of sin. So where does the believer in Jesus Christ turn in such difficult times? Is our faith sufficiently grounded in the truths of the Bible? Where do we seek comfort?

For the faithful servant, it must center in the end on Jesus Christ as our Suffering Servant who enters into our suffering with us (Isaiah 53; 1 Peter 2:21-24). He is both transcendent and personal. He will return to remove every tear from our eyes and end all suffering and pain from our sinful hearts as we live forever in sinless bliss with our God (Revelation 21:1-5; Philippians 3:8-9).

As previously noted, several in my church have significantly suffered from traumatic events of death in their families. Like nearly all pastors, I have held the hand of a dying saint who had been diagnosed with cancer from fighting in Vietnam. Families have wayward children. There is pain and suffering in every family and in every life.

Suffering is all around us. We live in a fallen world where sin has stained everything. People suffer. The statistics are staggering when you consider how many people suffer from violence, either in the home or in society. Financial ruin comes overnight as banks collapse or jobs evaporate. COVID-19 has left a mark on every aspect of our lives. Trust has eroded on every front. The way we present Christ in such times is a major part of our faithful witness.

People need to know how to handle such times of crisis. As believers in Jesus Christ, Christians need to be able to step up and help not only fellow believers but their lost neighbors and friends as well.[12] There is such a need to understand the character of God in such difficult times.

During the extended time of COVID-19 and the world pandemic, people continued to suffer. Who would have guessed that at the end of two years of this virus, there would be no end in sight? Much has been written about how this pandemic has changed our culture and the church. More will be revealed in the days ahead. There is a need to examine how we trust God when the foundations of life have been so damaged and life so interrupted. Churches continue to try and find a path forward. Pain abounds. Some have lost jobs. Others have not returned to church because of age, health-related issues, and or fear of the virus. People are tired and worn down. Into this dark place of despair, the gospel can bring hope, comfort, and encouragement. Just as Job looked for an answer to "why" he was suffering so much but instead found the "who" of all creation, so our communities need Christ more than ever before as they deal with this pervasive and heavy suffering. Just as Job saw that he must depend on God no matter his circumstances, so the church needs to help our congregants and communities flee to the comfort of Christ. We cannot just love God for what he provides in good times. Thomas Morton has written that if we love God for something that is less than just God Himself, we run the risk of never receiving what we hoped for. We can end up hating God because He does not match up to our expectations for Him.[13] Perhaps never in the recent history of the church has there been a greater need for the people of God to build the foundations to handle suffering and pain.

The purpose of this book is to engage others in a biblical understanding of how the Bible deals with suffering and, through that, to rebuild trust in our mighty God in a pandemic world. People need to know who and where God is and how His character operates during suffering.

Suffering often spotlights our emotional fragility and the fractures of our faith. Chaos will reveal our true focus and dependence when circumstances do not go according to our plan. A Christ-centered approach to pain and suffering brings joy in Jesus Christ (James 1:2).[14] While much has been written on suffering, I want to assimilate the multitude of information into five foundation stones that can be used to strengthen the faith of my readers.

There are five foundation stones for Christians to remember and stay grounded in during suffering:

1 — Source

2 — Sovereignty

3 — Shepherd

4 — Significance

5 — Surety.

The following five lessons will help to build these foundational stones for understanding and working through suffering. These include lessons on:

1 — The Problem of Sin and Suffering — The Loss of Trust

2 — God's Sovereignty and Suffering in the Old

Testament

3 — The Suffering Servant and the Cross

4 — The Purpose of Suffering

5 — Abandoned by God — A Pastoral Perspective for Suffering and Learning to Trust God

Under each topic, we will consider not only the biblical passages related to suffering, but also within each lesson we examine how Scripture is applicable to real-life suffering and loss. The Bible is very helpful in showing us how to support others from a Christian worldview as part of our being the hands and feet of Christ in our sphere of influence. This is the call of Christ to us as we live out our faith in the one who suffers with us.

Foundation Stone: Source

Lesson: The Problem of Sin and Suffering — The Loss of Trust

We will consider passages of Scripture from Genesis, Job, Jeremiah, 1 Kings, and Romans. Suffering surrounds us. As John Stott has written, "The fact of suffering undoubtedly constitutes the greatest challenge to the Christian faith and has been for every generation."[15] Suffering is not just an intellectual issue or a theoretical argument; suffering is very personal, and it often leaves us struggling to find firm ground to stand on as we become disoriented, angry, and frightened. The psalmist, Jeremiah, Habakkuk, Job, and Elijah all found suffering and the apparent triumph of evil more than they could handle at times. The emotionality of suffering can catch us off guard and sweep us away. We must have a firm foundation to stand on as the storms of life sweep over us. We will briefly examine how non-Christians view suffering. What is the theodicy of the atheist, the deist, and the pantheist?

The cost of sin is suffering and death. Between Genesis and Revelation, sin, suffering, and pain are found on almost every page. Sin entered the world at the Fall in the third chapter of Genesis, and we briefly examine the various covenants of God in light of the fact that man is a fallen creature. We study to see what Scripture says about all evil being moral evil. Further, we explore how the suffering of recent years has caused even Christians to see the cracks in their trust in God.

Foundation Stone: Sovereignty

Lesson: God's Sovereignty and Suffering in the Old Testament

God's sovereignty and the Book of Job are the focus of this lesson. We begin by looking at our foundation stone — God is all-powerful and all good all the time, yet evil and suffering exist. We can take what we have learned up to this point to begin building a biblical theodicy for suffering. Discussions center around God's sovereignty and man's moral responsibility. The story of Joseph in Genesis is one of the main passages that examines how God's providence is in total control, yet He does not let man off the hook for His sins.

We also can consider how various biblical characters learned to live trust-filled lives in the face of suffering. As we examine the Book of Job and the character of the man himself. We consider the doctrine of Retribution Theology, the conversations that Job had with his three friends, and the final conversation with Elihu. How did Job answer the accusations made against him, and how did he handle the overwhelming suffering that God allowed Satan to bring into his life? We will examine Job's call for a mediator between himself and God to bring justice to his cause. We can consider God's reply to Job and Job's response to God.

In relation to God's sovereignty, we will also examine the rest of the Old Testament in how it relates to the topic of suffering and trust in God. We will briefly consider the Lament Psalms and the help they can be to our emotional and spiritual struggles.

Further ideas center around the role of prayer within God's sovereignty. Can we pray for healing? Does prayer change God's mind? How can we keep our prayers centered on God's will and not our own? We conclude this session by examining the truth and strength of understanding God's sovereignty.

Foundation Stone: Shepherd

Lesson: The Suffering Servant and the Cross

As we study the Suffering Servant, we will focus on passages in Isaiah, 1 Peter, and Luke. To have a proper biblical view of suffering, we must start with an understanding of Christ, His mission, and His suffering. We discuss Christ's life with suffering, the doctrine of the cross, and the role of the cross in our daily lives. We need to understand that the God of our faith is worthy of that faith. We examine the justice and love of God that meet at the cross and how the resurrection confirms that work. In considering the imminence of God in our suffering, the lesson discusses how the work of Christ on the cross is the center of our suffering.

In studying Luke 9, we work our way through how we are to take up our cross daily in willingness to suffer for Jesus's sake. What does this mean for the mundane moments of our lives? How does suffering lead us to share in Christ's glory?

Foundation Stone: Significance

Lesson: The Purpose of Suffering

Examining significance leads us to look at specific biblical passages to build a case for the three main purposes of suffering. We will discuss how God uses suffering and pain as discipline for sin and personal sanctification and to reveal his glory while presenting the sufferer with a greater view of God. The section will consider a wide range of biblical passages. We begin by considering our lives within a fallen world. The question dealt with in this session will not be so much the question of "Why?" but of "For what end?" We will look at what the Bible says about discipline in the Christian life and how God often uses suffering to perfect our faith and our growth in holiness. Discussions center around how easy and quick answers for suffering often yield little fruit for our struggles. Romans 8:28 is an important part of the work.

One emphasis for this specific section is to see how the Bible never takes suffering lightly. God always has a purpose in our suffering. Within the discussion, we will read the testimony of Dr. James M. Boice on his last Sunday to his congregation at Tenth Presbyterian Church in Philadelphia, PA.

How do we once again trust in God's sovereignty when our world has permanently changed? How do we find solid footing in the middle of chaos? These are the questions of the person who suffers. Finally, we begin to point again to God's sovereignty as we try to view suffering in our present age from the vantage point of the end of our lives and the glory that awaits all God's children.

Foundation Stone: Surety

Lesson: Abandoned by God — A Pastoral Perspective for Suffering and Learning to Trust Christ Again

This final foundation stone considers how we often feel abandoned by God in our time of suffering, perhaps more acutely in a post-COVID-19 world. Yet we know from our foundation stones that we are not abandoned but squarely in the place that God has sovereignly ordained for us. Rebuilding trust in Christ after the COVID-19 pandemic is critical because so many have suffered. We will discuss the five foundation stones for suffering and consider pastoral and practical help for questions concerning suffering.

When considering the question of suffering, everyone brings some sort of worldview to the problem. This book is designed to help Christians build a coherent worldview on the subject of suffering. That suffering can be physical, emotional, or spiritual. In the remaining chapters, I will undertake to build a biblical theodicy for suffering in an effort to support other Christians who find themselves confused and unsure about their faith in such times.

As I write this book, my prayer is that God will use His biblical principles to strengthen the church and our communities with the power of the Holy Spirit. As we learn to build our lives on these foundation stones, I believe the truth that is found here should continue to spill over into other areas of our lives to bolster faith, renew hope, and draw us ever closer to Christ.

CHAPTER TWO

BIBLICAL AND THEOLOGICAL INSIGHTS INTO SUFFERING

The problem of pain and suffering has plagued mankind since the fallen world began. When Adam and Eve sinned, pain and suffering entered the world (Genesis 3:1-19). Suffering is all around us. Yet the pastor is called to shepherd his people through the valley of pain in a way that upholds God and meets people where they are in the middle of their existential crisis. This ministry requires a proper understanding of evil in the world, a solid foundational theology of suffering from God's Word, and a helpful skillset to meet the needs of those who suffer.

All humanity faces the problem of suffering, and so many ask the question, "Why?" How can we reconcile it all? Agnostic-turned-Christian Sheldon Vanauken states that everyone wants to know why the child dies of a brain tumor or the drunk driver kills the husband and child. He goes on to say that "a mention of God — of God's will does not help a bit."[16]

John Stott once wrote that the problem of pain and suffering was the single greatest challenge to the Christian faith when it appears to be so random and so out of sync with God's love and justice.[17] Suffering is not just an intellectual problem, but it is also, and more importantly for many, an intensely personal one. A person can feel anger, worry, and disoriented because it would appear that often the wicked seem to prosper while the righteous suffer (Jeremiah 12:1; Job 21:7-14.)

The Christian faith must hold three statements in tension because the Bible holds them in tension. God is all-powerful. God is all good. Evil exists in His world. Many Christians easily assent to these truths until trage- dy strikes. The fact that God is sovereign even over evil is part of the bedrock of the Christian faith.[18] But these foundational truths only serve to point us in the right di- rection of Jesus. Our comfort in times of pain and suffer- ing is Christ as our personal Savior.

Theology is how and what we think about God, and a theology of suffering or theodicy is how we think about God in times of crisis. Pain and suffering can funda- mentally change the spiritual and emotional health of a Christian.[19] In such times, the Christian naturally turns to the Bible to find encouragement, hope, and answers to the problem of suffering. The Old and New Testaments contain God's help and hope for those who suffer, and while the stories and teachings found there are God's perfect truth, ultimately, we will find our hope and help in the person and work of Jesus Christ. It is when we view the cross of Christ that we see our suffering servant who relates to us in our time of need.

Biblical Types of Suffering

Suffering never leaves a person as it found him or her. A person is always changed by suffering. You can be changed for the better, or you can be crushed under the weight of suffering. No one ever emerges from suffering without a new and different perspective on life.[20] There are many different types of suffering. Equally, there can be countless reasons for suffering. Job details some of these within the prose and poetry sections of the book. Caution should always be taken to discard the quick and simple answers about suffering.[21] A one-size-fits-all, tailored saying to someone in a time of need can only lead to more pain and suffering. We can think that we need to defend God in cases of incredible pain and loss, but the comforter often mistakenly treats the loss as an intellectual issue rather than a personal one.[22] Job's friends, who sit in silence for seven days with him, are helpful examples that the sufferer often just needs presence more than unhelpful words (Job 2:13).

Suffering always puts pressure on our faith. It will expose our weaknesses and take our eyes off Christ (Luke 8:7,14). Suffering has the ability to turn our focus away from Jesus and place it almost entirely on ourselves.[23] Yet in the midst of suffering, we should find ourselves leaning more and more on our relationship with God. This will be the ultimate message of Job, where God's wisdom and integrity are on trial, and no answers to Job's questions are forthcoming. We should never hesitate to trust the wisdom of God even when we have no answers to our "Why" questions and find ourselves groping in the dark.[24] In the Book of Job, God takes full responsibility for the suffering that Job endures, and Job and his friends never doubt that fact.[25] God's sovereignty is not questioned by Job or his friends, but the Almighty's wisdom and integrity are doubted as Job suffers mightily.

The Book of Job

Christians have naturally turned to the Book of Job because most people believe it is a book devoted to a theodicy of suffering. Theodicy can be defined as how an omnipotent and perfectly good God can create a world in which suffering exists, and why does he allow it to continue on such a prodigious scale? Job is a wonderful book of prose and poetry. By any standard of literature, it must rank among the most important works in the literature of the world.[26] Francis Anderson believes that Job is one of the greatest gifts ever given by God to the world. He rightly claims that it is broad in its ideas, comprehensive in its look at human emotions and experiences, and profound in its concept of God. The depths of human despair and moral outrage are on display in it. The apparent desertion of Job by God is on full display.[27]

Unfortunately, many people come away disappointed from reading Job because, while there is much to learn about suffering, the book is more about God's integrity and the source of wisdom. Suffering is the setting in which the discussion of God's wisdom takes place.[28] Job does not provide a comprehensive theodicy. The entire scope of Scripture does provide such a theodicy, but the Book of Job helps us to think about God and the types of suffering found in the world. For those looking to the book for answers to their questions as to how and why they suffer, Job will leave them disappointed and perhaps confused.[29] In reality, Job is about where wisdom is found and how can man really know God and trust His character. The suffering of Job is the crucible of life through which we learn much about the divine-human relationship.[30] The fact that God is sovereign over everything, including evil, is a foundational truth for the Christian faith.[31] Yet, in suffering, humanity cries out to ask how a good and omnipotent God can allow such heartache.

As has been previously stated, many commentators believe that the Book of Job is more concerned with God's wisdom and integrity than with Job's personal suffering. Certainly, Job's suffering is not redemptive in any way. Even his call for a mediator is for someone to argue his cause for vindication before God (Job 9:1-3).[32] His suffering serves as a platform for the topics of God's wisdom and our motivations for the pursuit of righteousness. God's integrity is what is on trial because He is the one who presents a righteous Job to the Accuser (Job 1:8).[33] God builds up Job and his righteousness. He does so in a heavenly court modeled on the ancient Near Eastern royal courts.[34] Job's righteousness is portrayed as extreme, just as his suffering will be. This idea of the conflict between Job's integrity and God's is vividly displayed in the book. Will Job curse God or stay in a relationship with Him?

The suffering Job endures comes from the dialogue between the Accuser and God. David J. A. Clines believes that God is the cosmic bully in this conversation, and Job bears the brunt of His violence as God hides His face from him.[35] Norman Habel suggests that the Accuser has "goaded God into a wager," causing God's very character to be on trial.[36] But neither of these is correct in their assessment of God. The real issue in the Book of Job is whether Job will worship God with a disinterested passion. Does he love God for God's sake alone or because of the blessings and gifts that God has bestowed on him?[37] If Job's relationship is based on the blessings he receives from God's hand, then he should curse God and abandon his relationship because God has apparently abandoned him. The Accuser would be proven right if Job follows this course (Job 1:9).[38] The beauty of the Book of Job, as George Schwab writes, is found in the fact that suffering and the discipleship of serving God are tied together and explored in the book.[39] This relationship between suffering and discipleship is illuminated through the words of the main characters in the book: Job, Eliphaz, Bildad, Zophar, Elihu, and God.

As the book opens and the heavenly court reports are given, God points out Job to the Accuser, and the conflict starts. Job, in one day, loses his children, his home, and all of his earthly possessions. Previous to this, Job had enjoyed an intimate relationship with God that few others in Scripture have enjoyed. His relationship mirrors, in many ways, the one that Moses and Enoch had with God. There is a deep friendship between the Creator and the creature. Job was a wise and respected elder in his area. Through his suffering, Job's commitment to God would be on display for all to see.[40] When Job has experienced this first round of great loss, he still considers God of no less value to worship than before (Job 1:21). After the Accuser comes again before the heavenly court and again states that Job serves God for his blessing of life, God allows the Accuser to inflict his body with great sores so that his suffering is inclusive of both mental and physical. In Job's next dialogue, after his three friends arrive, his words are much harsher as he curses the day of his birth. He cries out with a deeply wounded heart, wanting God to explain why he is suffering so much. While this can be cathartic for some, as a pastor, I cannot always point to this chapter as a way to address God. Job's words are harsh and biting.[41] D. A. Carson correctly says that Job's demand for God to present Himself and explain the suffering in Job's life is the cry of every believer who suffers for unknown reasons. Job wants to know what God is doing. Job seems to trust God enough to be honest with Him for no other reason than he loves God.[42]

Job's three friends next speak up in a running cycle of dialogue that covers much of the book. They represent the wisdom of the day. They believe that Job has sinned, and his suffering is the punishment for that sin, even though the reader knows Job is upright and righteous in God's sight. Their theology of suffering is best described as retribution theology, where sin and punishment are directly tied to each other, often in an immediate way, and righteousness and blessing are equally directly connected. The righteous will always prosper, and the wicked will always suffer. These friends have no category to consider that God might not be just, and so they believe Job has sinned.[43] There is some basis for this idea set within the Old Testament covenants of blessings for obedience and curses for disobedience (Deuteronomy 28). Their efforts to persuade Job to confess his sins and be restored are based on their belief that retribution theology is always correct.[44] They see no room for any other idea as a basis for suffering. Job cannot accept this blanket judgment because he knows his own heart. He cannot support the idea that all suffering is tied to specific sin, and so he begins to question God's justice to him. He calls out God to come and present Himself to Job, knowing that he will be cleared. Instead, God appears to hide His face from Job.

It is interesting that Job's friends talk about God, and Job is the one who talks to God (Job 7:12-21, 9:28-31, 17:4).[45] Job does not ask for restoration but for vindication by God. This stance by Job shows that he is serving God with a disinterested passion and faith. He fears God and shuns evil because of his love for God and not the benefits he receives (Job 28:28).

After a wonderful wisdom poem in chapter 28 and Job's final call for vindication, a new character, Elihu, appears in the story. His sudden appearance seems to catch the reader by surprise, and his speech to Job serves as a transition to God's appearance to Job. Elihu takes a slightly different stance to suffering than the previous three friends. Commentators vary on how Elihu is viewed, ranging from a young upstart who adds nothing to the conversation to a wonderful, fresh voice defending God. Elihu has very specific thoughts on suffering as it relates to retribution theology. He argues that instead of suffering being the punishment for past sins, suffering can be in anticipation of future sins. Elihu believes Job is self-righteous in his attacks on God, and therefore, he has suffered in anticipation of that sin. Judgment may precede the sinful act itself.[46]

Larry Waters finds four main categories of suffering in Elihu's speeches. First, he writes that suffering is a preventative measure. Suffering keeps us from sinning in that it warns and instructs us. It can be used to turn people away from temptation and help to keep the sufferer humble. Second, he sees suffering as a corrective. Job was self-righteous and needed to be convicted of that sin. In addition, Waters argues that suffering is an educational tool. The sufferer can learn lessons from his or her pain.

Finally, he sees in Elihu's speeches a form of suffering that is used to bring glory to God.[47]

God finally speaks to Job out of the storm in the closing chapters of the book and tells Job to brace himself for what is about to happen (Job 38:1-2). God reveals, in His questions to Job, His magnificent glory and wisdom. Here, many readers are frustrated because God fails to answer Job's specific questions about vindication. God speaks of His wisdom in the cosmic realm of creation and the earthly animal kingdom. His questions to Job reveal God's wisdom, power, and righteousness. Antony Campbell makes a strange argument that God directs Job to an alternate reality for suffering in the animal realm because it is amoral. For Campbell, suffering in the animal kingdom is simply bad luck or "nature's lottery." Causation is never needed.[48] For a God who is completely sovereign, luck has no place in creation or suffering.

Faith reasserts itself in Job after God speaks to him. In addressing Job, God brings him dignity and a humble sense of purpose.[49] Job ends up with no answers to why he is suffering but is content to accept what God has given him.[50] He finally realizes that God's ways and thoughts are higher than his understanding (Isaiah 55:9). For Job, the ultimate answer is that he sees God and realizes his relationship is built on grace. God's speech has moved Job from self-focus to a focus on God.[51] Job now understands that God is found in a dependent relationship with him as wisdom replaces suffering as the theme of the book.[52] Job sees that he must depend on God no matter his circumstances. The goal in undeserved and mysterious suffering is to hold on to God and to seek His presence. Thomas Morton writes that if we love God for something that is less than just God Himself, we run the risk of never receiving what we hoped for. We can end up hating God because He does not match up to our expectations of Him.[53]

Sometimes, there is no direct correlation between suffering and personal sin. To realize that God owes us no explanation and that He is supremely wise, even in the face of great suffering, is to receive comfort from Him. God is always sovereign, even in the chaotic times of life. He is sovereign over evil itself.[54] We trust Him because He is God. He is never surprised or caught off guard.

Suffering in the Old Testament

While the Book of Job delivers a strong rebuttal to the idea that retribution theology is always correct in every situation, the idea is not unique to that book alone. Additionally, the Old Testament helps Christians to understand

a variety of concepts surrounding suffering. The covenants of the Old Testament between biblical characters or
the nation of Israel and God all had curses and blessings
associated with obedience and disobedience (Deuteronomy 27, 28). The prophets issued oracles containing punishment on the people if they violated God's requirements
(Amos 4:6-12).[55] Certainly, the idea of covenant, while
not mentioned in the Book of Job, is presupposed.[56]

Job's genre is wisdom literature and, therefore, has
much in common with Proverbs and Ecclesiastes in that
all three books highlight the search for wisdom. Ronald
Hesselgrave argues that all three books show that wisdom
can only be found in God. Job and Qoheleth struggle with
questions of faith when their understanding of retribution
theology does not match personal experience.[57]

The Psalms play an important role in understanding suffering and faith, mostly through the role of the
Lament Psalms. This is the largest category of the Book
of Psalms. There are more than sixty Lament Psalms that
come to us in the form of either personal or Corporate
Laments. Individual laments often deal with personal
persecution, such as Psalms 3, 4, 5, 17, and 27. Other
individual laments deal with sickness, such as Psalms
6, 13, 22, and 30-32.[58] While Job and the laments found

in Psalms share some common themes, Daniel Timmer accurately explains the difference between the literary forms found in the two books. In Psalms, the author speaks truthfully about God. Many of the Lament Psalms contain addresses to God in personal lament where there is an affirmation of who God is and the author's unyielding trust in God's character. Usually, these psalms end in some sort of praise. Job's speeches do not contain many of these characteristics. His reflection on God's character, which is praised in the Lament Psalms, is challenged in Job as he calls into question God's justice.[59] The writer of many of the Psalms seems to believe in retribution theology as well (Psalm 69). But Psalms, better than Job, helps the sufferer in being honest with God and crying out in pain. In Psalms, there seems to be a trust in the character of God that is missing from Job's speeches prior to God speaking to him from the whirlwind. Job calls for a mediator to argue his case against God (Job 9:33). This is not a messianic mediator but an angel to support his case against God, to vindicate him before God. It is often the cry of the believer today in the middle of pain and suffering. Corporate Lament Psalms are cries for the community. They, too, can be cries for past sins, but in terms of the nation, they are more so than the individual, as in Psalms 44, 60, 74, and 123.[60] But the Old Testament is full of real messianic cries for one to come and save His people (Isaiah 55).

Certainly, there are many other Old Testament characters who demonstrate to believers how to live faithful, trusting lives during times of acute suffering and trials. Shadrach, Meshach, and Abednego endure the wrath of King Nebuchadnezzar for their singular worship of God instead of the King. Their persecution, like that of many of the reformers, was to be burned alive. They stand firm in their unyielding faith that God will either deliver them out of the fire or through the fire (Daniel 3:8-30). They were willing to yield up their bodies in service to God and serve as faithful models even in the face of death.[61] Later in Daniel's life, again, he models faithfulness in the lion's den. In the face of an evening with hungry lions, he goes to the Lord in prayer during his trials. Even though in both of these stories from the Book of Daniel, God delivered these men unharmed, the point of the stories for Christians today is not that God will always bring about the results we want but that these men show us how to be faithful in the middle of suffering.

No Old Testament biblical character illustrates for us the role of human responsibility and the sovereignty of God in suffering better than Joseph (Genesis 37, 39-50).

Joseph suffers mightily under the weight of his brothers' wrath for his dreams of rule over them. Eventually, this jealousy of the older brothers leads them to sell him to the Midianites, who sell him into slavery in Egypt. For many years, while Joseph follows God faithfully, his circumstances find him in prison in Egypt. There, forgotten and without hope, God is molding him in the chaos of his life to be the man God wants him to be so that he can one day rule Egypt under Pharaoh during the famine. After his father died, his brothers, who had sold him into slavery, became worried that Joseph would take revenge on them. But Joseph gives us that great verse that sets up the beauty of the sovereignty of God even in their sinful actions when he says to them, "You intended to harm me, but God intended it for good, to accomplish what is now being done, the saving of many lives" (Genesis 50:20). Much more could be said about how Moses suffered in the wilderness for forty years as God prepared him to lead the people out in the Exodus (Acts 7:30). Or how Elijah learned the lessons of complete dependence on God in the midst of suffering as the ravens fed him morning and evening and he drank from the brook Cherith (1 Kings 17:1-7).

Within the context of the grand narrative of God's story, the Old Testament contributes much to the arena of suffering, but it is not until we come to the New Testament that we can truly appreciate Job's ending, and our real mediator arrives.

Suffering in the New Testament

When Christians come to the New Testament, we find that the idea of retribution theology still permeated the Jewish culture as the theology of suffering. Suffering and pain were always a part of life in Jesus's day. Jesus confronts this in John 9 when He is with His disciples and a blind man is there. His disciples think the man was born blind because of some sin he did or something his parents might have done. In this situation, Jesus offers a new lesson in suffering that, I believe, actually tracks somewhat in Job. Jesus tells His disciples that the man was born blind so that on that specific day, Jesus could heal him and thus show God's glory. Here, we see purpose in suffering. The purpose of this man suffering from blindness was so that people could see God's glory in his healing. It was all part of God's sovereign plan and is the same wisdom and glory that was displayed to Job by God's questions.[62] We see this same understanding of retribution theology in Luke 13, where a building had fallen and killed many people. Here, the suffering cannot be tied to a specific sin. Again, Jesus shifts the focus from retribution theology to purpose. As believers in Jesus Christ read the

New Testament, we see that Jesus never promises a life free from pain and suffering. Quite the contrary, He says to take up our cross and follow Him (Matthew 10:38-39). Paul echoes these same thoughts when he talks about his own suffering in 2 Corinthians. The idea of suffering as a part of the believer's life is everywhere in the books of the New Testament (Romans 8:18; James 1:2-5; 1 Peter 1:6; Hebrews 2:10).

In 1 Peter, the central theme is suffering. The letter is addressed to those who are suffering during the Jewish Diaspora and is meant to encourage them and give them hope. Trials are temporary, and there is a purpose in their suffering that will bring a refining fire to their faith. While they suffer unjustly, God's providence always triumphs over evil. God is personally involved in our suffering. While He permits and therefore ordains their persecution, suffering Christians are allowed to join with Christ in His suffering (1 Peter 2:21).[63] The Apostle Peter goes on to call us to glorify God in our suffering (1 Peter 4:12-19). Finally, God's grace is always sufficient to sustain us in all our suffering. He alone can provide abiding strength (1 Peter 5:10).[64]

The Apostle Paul was no stranger to suffering (2 Corinthians 11:16-33). One of his strongest statements on suffering in and for Christ comes to us in his letter to the Philippian Church. In his epistle, he writes that suffering is a gift that is granted to us by God for Christ's sake to accompany our faith (Philippians 1:29). Suffering as a gift is a difficult concept to accept, much less embrace.

What the Book of Job left unfinished, regarding suffering, is solved in the divine justice of the cross. Jesus is the ultimate solution to pain and suffering. In a relationship with Him, we do not always find answers to "Why," but we do find the answer to "Who" and purpose.[65] Some have seen Job as a prefigure of Christ, but there are too many differences to make that comparison. Walton and Longman point out that any comparison highlights the differences more than the similarities. Job suffers involuntarily, while Jesus voluntarily goes to the cross. Job accused God; Jesus obeyed Him. Job's suffering has a didactic purpose for the Book of Job; Christ's suffering and death were redemptive for all who believe.[66]

However, there is some common ground that should be pointed out. The Book of Job highlights the aseity, sovereignty, and wisdom of God. These characteristics are shown perfectly in the person and work of Jesus Christ.[67] The life of Christ shows us that God is not apart from our suffering even when we cannot see Him. He is never just a spectator but participates with us in our pain and suffering. Struggles with chaos in the lives of humanity are displayed from Genesis to Revelation. The Fall caused all of humanity and nature to tumble into sickness and death (Genesis 3). Sin is rebellion against God.[68] Suffering will always be a part of life because of our sin and because we follow Christ. But one day, suffering and pain will end when our Savior returns (Revelation 7:17, 21:4).

The Price of Sin

One of the main foundation stones in dealing with the problem of pain and suffering is the price of sin. Between Genesis and Revelation in the Bible is pain, suffering, and sin. Evil battles against God's goodness and mercy. The Fall caused both humanity and nature to tumble from the realm of good into sickness and death (Genesis 3). As Philip Yancey writes, creation itself is bent. "Nature is our fallen sister and not our mother." [69] Sin is rebellion against God.[70] There is, however, a distinction between moral evil and natural evil that needs to be understood. There is a difference between a murder (moral evil) and a hurricane (natural evil). While both are the result of sin and are evil, a distinction needs to be made between the two. People suffer from both types of evil.[71]

Because we live in a fallen world, Christians do

suffer. We will suffer for our faith because of our sin and because we live in a fallen world. It is inescapable.[72] Suffering can also come from false expectations. We think that we do not deserve the hand God deals us. This false understanding is driven by a works theology where people believe that they have lived a "good" life and should enjoy ease and comfort. This is especially true in the Western world. But sin deserves the wrath of God (Romans 3:10-12, 6:23). When we manage our expectations and know that suffering will come, we are better able to lean into Jesus (John 16:33). In addition, we are less likely to blame God for our suffering when we manage our expectations. As I shepherd my flock, we have to recognize tragedies are personal and seriously painful, yet recognize God's sovereignty in it all. Christians know the beauty of grace when they recognize their sin and have suffered in this world.

Suffering and pain are the price of sin. While not all pain is because of sin, suffering is a result of the Fall. As I teach, I often make the point that we suffer because we love sin more than God. In America, we often try to move on too quickly from our times of sin, taking God's forgiveness for granted rather than doing the hard work of self-examination. We want things to get better for us, so we try to bury our sins and take shortcuts in our spiritual work.[73] We must also guard against retribution theology. This heresy occurs when we think that each and every time we suffer, it is necessarily tied to a specific sin.[74] Job's friends believed in retribution theology (Job 8:6). The Bible does teach that we reap what we sow (Galatians 6:7). However, the Bible also clearly teaches that we cannot connect each time we suffer to a specific sin. I often teach my congregation the story of the man born blind (John 9:1-12). In that story, Jesus talks about how suffering can be for God's glory. This heretical doctrine of retribution theology is used when we try to comfort our friends in their time of need. Nothing can be more damaging. Yes, sin has consequences, but we cannot always know the direct relationship between our sin and our suffering. In ministry, the price of sin must be understood to make sense out of suffering and pain.

I want to return briefly here to the question I am most often asked, "Why?" It is the cry of the desperate heart. The heart wants to know why God is allowing this or if He is even there.[75] One of the hardest topics that I find to teach is the lesson on God's discipline. The most dominant form of suffering in the Bible for believers is that of being disciplined by God. I find at least four identifiable lessons in Scripture that help people sometimes understand the "Why" question. First, God disciplines

us in times of pain and suffering to help us combat sin
(2 Corinthians 12:7).[76] The history of Israel speaks to
this lesson. Often, they are punished because they have
failed to follow God. The Book of Judges is a cycle of sin
followed by punishment, repentance, and restoration. The
cycle then repeats. Second, God often uses suffering and
pain to encourage us in our faith and to perfect our faith
(1 Peter1:3-9; John 15:1-2). He prunes us to cause us to
produce more fruit. Third, God uses our times of struggle
to train us to persevere in our faith. He calls us to stay
strong in the face of hardship (Romans 5:1-5). Lastly, I
relay to my congregation that God often uses these times
of discipline to confirm to us that we are indeed His children (Proverbs 3:11-12; Hebrews 12:8). We may never
know for sure in all cases if our time of suffering and
pain is of God to discipline us or if we struggle simply
because we live in a fallen world. We do not always need
to decide or know for sure what God is doing in our lives.
We simply must trust in the Lord (Proverbs 3:5). But we
never escape God's sovereignty.[77] James Boice certainly
echoed this truth the last time he addressed his congregation in Philadelphia. He reminded his congregation that
God is sovereign and that they should pray for God to be
glorified in all of his suffering. Instead of asking for the
reason, he states, "If God does something in your life,

would you change it? If you would change it, you would make it worse. It wouldn't be as good. So that is the way we want to accept it and move forward, and who knows what God will do."[78] This is a mighty lesson for anyone. The following poem speaks to God's work in the lives of his children. I often use it when talking about the works of God in our lives.

> When God wants to drill a man
>   And thrill a man
>   And skill a man,
> When God wants to mold a man
>   To play the noblest part;
> When He yearns with all His heart
>   To create so great and bold a man
> That all the world shall be amazed,
>   Watch His methods, watch His ways!
> How He ruthlessly perfects
>   Whom He royally elects!
> How He hammers him and hurts him,
>   And with mighty blows converts him
> Into trial shapes of clay which
>   Only God understands;
> While his tortured heart is crying
>   And he lifts beseeching hands!
> How He bends but never breaks
>   When his good He undertakes;
> How He uses whom He chooses
>   And with every purpose fuses him;
>   By every act induces him
> To try His splendour out
>   God knows what He›s about!
>   (Author Unknown)[79]

Christ and Suffering

Does Christ care about our suffering? Two passages in the Gospels can cause us to wonder if He really does care or not. In Mark 4, the disciples are in a boat crossing the Sea of Galilee when a storm threatens to swamp the boat and drown these seasoned fishermen. Jesus is asleep in the stern (Mark 4:35-41). The disciples go to Him crying out, saying, "Teacher, don't you not care if we drown?" The disciples seem to have the attitude that He doesn't care because He is simply asleep during their great time of need. The other passage could equally raise the same question.

The other story from Jesus's life concerns his dear friend Lazarus. In John's Gospel, we get the story of the death of Lazarus (11:1-44). The disciple that Jesus loved writes that when Jesus heard the news of Lazarus's sickness, He did not leave immediately but waited two more days before going to him (11:6). We might ask why He delayed. We most certainly know that Jesus loved Lazarus and that He was healing many people in the land. Yet He stayed in His current location for two more days. When He does arrive, Lazarus's sisters, Mary and Martha, are both suffering grief and pain from their loss. Additionally, they are hurt that their friend did not arrive in time to prevent their hurt and pain. Did Jesus not care?

Well, we know from Scripture that both stories ended well. The storm was calmed, and Lazarus was raised from the dead. God was glorified in both events. But the lesson is critical here. God's glory is more important than anything else. God works on his own timeline and not ours. The joy we should take from these events is that Jesus does care. He rebukes the storm. He weeps with Mary and Martha. But, ultimately, He will show He cares at Golgotha.[80]

On the cross, Christ pays the price for all of our personal sins. He feels them as He hangs there. His beloved Father turns His back on the Son He loves.[81] To truly begin to build a foundation for understanding suffering and to minister to those in need, I always lead my people to the cross and the Suffering Servant of Isaiah (Isaiah 53; Luke 9:18-24; 1 Peter 2:21-24). Christ's suffering brings light to the issue of personal suffering. It helps us to put these events that crush us into perspective. Christ suffered the ultimate pain of our sins to bring us salvation. It was the perfect love of God that placed Him there.[82] There are three main points in studying the cross as it relates to the problem of pain and suffering. The first point is that the cross is an expression of our own sinful hearts. It represents the rebellion of sin against God and my anger toward Him and His truth. Our sins hold Him on the cross, and He willingly bears it out of love. Second, the cross represents forgiveness and restoration of our broken relationship because of sin. In our pain and sorrow, it is at the cross where we begin to rebuild our relationship with Him as Savior and Lord through the power of the Holy Spirit working in our hearts and minds (2 Corinthians 5:21; Romans 12:2). The third point in connection with the cross is that it shows us in vivid detail that God is not distant from us in our time of suffering and pain. Suffering is very personal for Him as Christ Himself dies for us (Hebrews 2:14-18; Romans 8:32). God stands with us in the midst of our suffering. This fact can be so important to people in their struggles when their hearts cry out to God. While it is a hard lesson to learn in the middle of suffering, it is a foundational truth that supports us in our times of trouble. His love surrounds and upholds us. D. A. Carson writes that when we cannot see any evidence that God loves us in the darkest of times, the Christian needs to look to the cross for proof that he loves us eternally.[83] We are called to join Christ in his suffering (James 1:12; 1 Peter 4:13). When we suffer in this life for His sake, we are linked to His suffering. The cross gives us context for our suffering.

The End View

The joyful hope of every Christian life is eternity with God. This hope is the filter through which we are able to handle suffering. We can build foundational blocks of faith to be prepared for suffering and pain when we keep our eyes on the ultimate goal of eternal life.[84] For many Christians, they see the end of time when Christ returns as a time of vindication and judgment for the suffering they and others have endured (1 Corinthians 13:12; Acts 10:42). From the end perspective, we will see and understand much of what has mystified us here in this life. The Bible gives us this perspective, and I lead my people to try and hold on to it (Revelation 21:1-5). Our sufferings will not compare to the joy we have in heaven (Romans 8:18). Our lives here on earth are not made for our happiness, security, or comfort but for God's glory (Philippians 3:8-9). God is truly working out all things for our good, even though we may not see it or feel it. We must hold on by faith to knowing it and knowing Christ (Romans 8:28).

There are several themes when considering the end view of suffering and pain. First, Christians should develop a homesickness for heaven (1 Peter 5:10).[85] One of the purposes of suffering and pain is to cause the Christian to long for heaven. We strive in suffering for an eternal perspective. By looking at suffering from the long view, we know that Christ meets us in the midst of our suffering and that this is not the end. Our current suffering and pain are not the last words on the matter. Jesus Christ is and has the last word as he makes all things new, as we keep our minds on heavenly things.[86] The next lesson I see in viewing pain and suffering from the end is that we know heaven is our home, and Jesus Christ is our hope. Mankind can offer no answers for the darkest days of our lives (Psalm 146:2-3). Another theme is how death becomes much less daunting when viewed from eternity. It becomes not the end but the beginning. J. I. Packer has noted, "Health and life, I would say, in the full and final sense of these words, are not what we die out of, but what we die into."[87]

I remember giving a speech to the students in grades six through twelve at Gaston Christian School after I had been cleared of my cancer. I gave my testimony and the Bible verses that had helped me and thanked them for the prayers, cards, and support they had given me. At the end of the time as I was speaking to the students as they went back to class, one young lady in the ninth grade came up to me and commented that she was glad I was better now. Then, her next words left me almost speechless. "My mom had cancer too, but she died." At that moment, all I could stumble out was to tell her that God heals in many ways. From that moment, some eighteen years ago, I still vividly remember her and her words. Even with an eternal perspective, suffering is still very personal. Finally, I think an end view of suffering helps to give us a basis for our prayers, both for ourselves and others.

It was important to note to my seminar group that understanding evil and suffering from an end view does not solve our immediate problem of pain and suffering. It will help to adjust our expectations. But for those who do not believe in Christ, the Bible offers no hope and no answers to this problem.[88] Christians must understand the notion of the already but not yet realization of the Kingdom of God.

The end view can also help us in this life. While I will speak to this more later, I can honestly say that my time of suffering with cancer was the most spiritually helpful time of my life. While I would never wish the gift of cancer on anyone, for it is a horrible disease, I can honestly echo Muggeridge's words. God used that time to break me of pride, self-centeredness, and self-confidence in my own abilities. I remember the very night when I told God I had nothing left to fight this disease, that I was done. I can still hear my wife trying to feed three small children in the kitchen and thinking of her going on without me. It was as if God yelled at me in that moment. "Finally, you are empty of self, so I can now start to fill you with my Spirit." While not audible, it was clear. I had reached the end of my hoarded resources.[89] My life now bears the scars and benefits of my suffering from cancer, and I am a better Christian because of that time. But a time is coming when Jesus will wipe away every tear, and there will be no more suffering or pain, and He will make all things new (Revelation 21:4-5)!

COVID-19 and Suffering

Suffering has surrounded us all. Who would have guessed that now, after more than two years, there would be no end to the spread in sight? Church services have had to change; depression, suicide, and a sense of frustration and fear grip my community. Much has been written about the virus and how it is changing our culture and society. This is a type of suffering from the Book of Job because there seems to be no reason for the sickness and death that has touched every area. Like Job, we often ask the wrong question. Job wanted to know "Why" he was afflicted since he was a righteous man.

The church seems loath to discuss the judgment of God as it relates to any type of widespread suffering. One only has to think of the horrible tsunami that swept over Southeast Asia in the year 2004 or the events of September 11, 2001, in New York City and Washington, DC. N. T. Wright writes that the church should avoid quick and pat answers to pain and suffering on such a worldwide scale. He reminds us that the Psalms of Lament do not give answers to the question of "Why" but do provide hope for us all (Psalms 6, 13, 22, 89).[90] As William Edgar says, Christians believe in judgment but never want to talk much about it. Yet in such times, followers of Jesus Christ should rightly lament. He reminds Christians that we do not possess all the answers, but we can and should ask God to intervene. As the Psalmist does in Psalm 80, we can cry out to God in confidence that He holds all the answers, and we can worship Him.[91]

Some have cried out asking, 'Where is God during this pandemic?' When we do not get answers to "Why" and we cry out to God even in lament, is He really there? N. T. Wright quotes the powerful poem by Malcolm Guite that was penned during Easter in 2020 when churches were closed, people were sheltering in place, and human contact was rare outside our own family.

> And where is Jesus, this strange Easter day?
> Not lost in our locked churches, anymore
> Than he was sealed in that dark sepulcher.
> The locks were loosed; the stone rolled away,
> And he is up and risen, long before,
> Alive, at large, and making his strong way
> Into the world he gave his life to save,
> No need to seek him in his empty grave.

He might have been a wafer in the hands
Of priest this day, or music from the lips:
Of red-robed choristers, instead he slips
Away from church, shakes off our linen bands
To don his apron with a nurse: he grips
And lifts a stretcher, soothes with gentle hands
The frail flesh of the dying, gives them hope,
Breathes with the breathless, lends them strength
to cope.

On Thursday we applauded, for he came
And served us in a thousand names and faces
Mopping our sickroom floors and catching traces
Of that corona which was death to him:
Good Friday happened in a thousand places
Where Jesus held the helpless, died with them
That they might share his Easter in their need,
Now they are risen with him, risen indeed.

Where is God during the COVID-19 pandemic? The answer, of course, is that He lives within those fellow Christians who shoulder our suffering with us. He is always there, always at work, always ministering in and through His brothers and sisters. Times of suffering are always an opportunity to bring the hope of the gospel to a dying world.[92]

Even in the midst of COVID-19, the solution to our suffering is Jesus and a growing relationship with Him. As a pastor, I count it a privilege to minister in such un-precedented days. In times of pain and suffering, Christ's love shines brightest, drawing people to Himself. The pandemic has brought much pain and suffering for the body of Christ and the world.

Scripture makes plain three statements about suffering and evil. It says that God is good. He is omnipotent. Evil and suffering exist. While these three facts seem to be in conflict, the Bible makes it clear that they can all be held in tension with each other. Indeed, Scripture teaches all three. In our fallen world, we will never be able to understand suffering and evil without a biblical theodicy.

CHAPTER THREE

FOUNDATION STONE: SOURCE

THE PROBLEM OF SIN AND SUFFERING — THE LOSS OF TRUST

What I hope to do in these foundation stone chapters is to give you foundational truths from God's Word that will help you understand suffering and strengthen your faith during the inevitable times you will struggle. We will look at building an infrastructure for working our way through suffering in a post-pandemic world by utilizing the five stones in our foundation. These five stones are Source, Sovereignty, Shepherd, Significance, and Surety. In these chapters, we will first learn where suffering originates, why it is all around us, and how it can cause us to question our trust in God. Second, we will consider who God is and how He interacts with us in sin and suffering. Third, we will look to Jesus and the Cross. He is our suffering servant. What does that mean for us? Fourth, we will consider the purposes of suffering. Is there an answer to the question of "why?" Is there meaning in our pain, or is it simply a random act of fate?

As we examine the fifth stone, we will honestly talk about how we can feel abandoned by God in times of pain and suffering. We will consider how we can rebuild trust in a post-Christian, pandemic world where the foundations of faith around us have seemingly been destroyed. The book will conclude with some very practical ways you can weather suffering and ways you can be a comfort to others in times of need.

As D. A. Carson has said, we must build a solid foundation for suffering when the winds and seas of life are calm. It is impossible to build footings in the middle of a hurricane. We need to learn these lessons now because suffering will come. My hope and prayer are that what I write about here will strengthen your faith and that when the storms of life come, and they will, your house will be built on the solid rock of our faithful God.

Our first foundation stone is Source.

The Problem of Sin and Suffering — The Loss of Trust.

Where does Suffering come from? Pain, chaos, anxiety, grief, shattered hopes and dreams, death, natural disasters, terrorism, and a world-wide pandemic - suffering is all around us. Sometimes, it is distant, only a repeating news story we hear on television or read on social media. At other times, it is real, personal, debilitating, and overwhelming. Nobody likes to talk about it, and yet it is, for some people, a lifelong companion. For others, it is a thief that comes unexpectedly in the night to rob us of any sense of normalcy. Suffering never leaves us the same as it found us. It will always change you in ways you can never imagine.

A couple spends thirty years working hard, paying off their mortgage, saving their money, and being a good church family. One day, the wife walks in and tells her husband that she is leaving him for another man. A common, everyday surgery turns complicated, and death calls unexpectedly to steal our loved one. Depression, addiction, and isolation lead a person to take his own life when no one ever saw it coming. A boss tells a worker that because of COVID-19 and the economic recession, his or her job has been eliminated. Suffering strikes every family.

We see this vividly played out in Job 1:13-19:

> One day when Job's sons and daughters were feasting and drinking wine at the oldest brother's house, a messenger came to Job and said, "The oxen were plowing and the donkeys were grazing nearby, and the Sabeans attacked and carried

them off. They put the servants to the sword, and I am the only one who has escaped to tell you!"

While he was still speaking, another messenger came and said, "The fire of God fell from the sky and burned up the sheep and the servants, and I am the only one who has escaped to tell you!"

While he was still speaking, another messenger came and said, "The Chaldeans formed three raiding parties and swept down on your camels and carried them off. They put the servants to the sword, and I am the only one who has escaped to tell you!"

While he was still speaking, yet another messenger came and said, "Your sons and daughters were feasting and drinking wine at the oldest brother's house, when suddenly a mighty wind swept in from the desert and struck the four corners of the house. It collapsed on them, and they are dead, and I am the only one who has escaped to tell you!"

In one day, Job loses all of his family and worldly possessions. We could also look at the verses in 1 Kings 21, where Queen Jezebel simply has a neighbor named Naboth killed because her husband, King Ahab, wants Naboth's vineyard, and he will not sell it. Evil is everywhere. It is woven into the fabric of our lives and society. Riots, senseless looting, and shootings seem to be the norm of the day.

There are three biblical truths that we can hold up during all suffering. First, God is All Powerful. Second, God is All Good. Third, Evil and Suffering Exist. This is a challenge to the Christian who looks in the face of grief and tries to hold on to these beliefs. British theologian John Stott writes that suffering constitutes the single greatest challenge to the Christian faith because it seems so random and therefore unfair." How can we hold God's love and justice in tension?[93]

We cry out, "Why." "Where is God?" How can a good God let any of this happen? Suffering leaves us disoriented and often frightened. We become angry with God. We may agree with the statements of God's goodness and power. But it can be truly hard to hold on and accept in the middle of chaos. How we view God and suffering is called "theodicy." We all have a worldview about suffering. These chapters should help you form a more coherent, relevant, and biblical theodicy.

The pollster George Barna asked, in a national survey, "If you could ask God only one question and you knew He would answer, what would you ask?" The top answer was, "Why is there pain and suffering in this world?"

There is a cute story attributed to Teresa of Avila where it is told that she falls off her carriage one day into a mud puddle. Wet and dirty, she cried out, "God why did you allow that to happen?" God replies, "This is the way I treat all my friends." Teresa then retorted, "Then, Lord, it is not surprising that you have so few."

Suffering happens to us all. Indeed the 20th Century was one of the bloodiest times of human history. What adds insult to injury is that it seems the wicked prosper. As the prophet Jeremiah cries out to God, "Why does the way of the wicked prosper? Why do all the faithless live at ease?" (Jeremiah 12:1).

So, where does suffering come from? If God is not the author of evil, where did suffering enter into a world that God had pronounced "very good" at the end of Genesis chapter one? God had given Adam one command of obedience, "You are free to eat from any tree in the garden; but you must not eat from the tree of the knowledge of good and evil, for when you eat of it you will surely die" (Genesis 2:16-17). If we read on to Genesis 3:8-19, we will see the answer in vivid detail as to where suffering comes from.

> Then the man and his wife heard the sound of the Lord God as he was walking in the garden in the cool of the day, and they hid from the Lord God among the trees of the garden. But the Lord God called to the man, "Where are you?" He answered, "I heard you in the garden, and I

was afraid because I was naked; so I hid."
And he said, "Who told you that you were na-
ked? Have you eaten from the tree that I com-
manded you not to eat from?"
The man said, "The woman you put here with me
- she gave me some fruit from the tree, and I ate
it."
Then the Lord God said to the woman, "What is
this you have done?"
The woman said, "The serpent deceived me, and
I ate."
So the Lord God said to the serpent, "Because you
have done this,
"Cursed are you above all livestock
    and all the wild animals!
You will crawl on your belly
    and you will eat dust
    all the days of your life.
And I will put enmity
    between you and the woman,
    and between your offspring and hers;
he will crush your head,
    and you will strike his heel."
To the woman he said,
"I will greatly increase your pains in childbearing;
    with pain you will give birth to children.
Your desire will be for your husband,
    and he will rule over you."
To Adam he said, "Because you listened to your
wife and ate from the tree about which I com-
manded you, 'You must not eat from it,'
"Cursed is the ground because of you;
    through painful toil you will eat of it
    all the days of your life.
It will produce thorns and thistles for you,

and you will eat the plants of the field.
By the sweat of your brow
   you will eat your food
until you return to the ground,
   since from it you were taken;
for dust you are
   and to dust you will return."

The Apostle Paul echoes God's judgment when he writes in Romans 6:23, "For the wages of sin is death, but the gift of God is eternal life in Christ Jesus our Lord." Between Genesis 3 and Revelation 21, pain and suffering exist throughout the biblical story. Sin is the cause of suffering.

When Adam and Eve sinned against God in an event we call The Fall, sin entered the world and all of creation. Through our first parent, Adam, sin is now inherent in every human being. Creation itself bears the marks and scars of sin and fallenness. As we read the Bible, we find sin, suffering, and tragedy in one story after another. The psalmists, Jeremiah, Job, Habakkuk, and Elijah all find suffering more than they can handle. What is evil or sin? Question twenty-four of the Larger Catechism of the Westminster Confession of Faith defines sin as "any want of conformity unto, or transgression of, any law of God." It is simply a rebellion against God. Adam and Eve rebelled against God in open disobedience. The Bible tells us that the result of open rebellion is spiritual death and a fallen existence in life.

Simply put, suffering happens because of sin. But let me quickly add that not all pain and suffering are the result of or tied to a specific sin. That often-distorted doctrine is called Retribution Theology, and we know that it is a false idea from Jesus's healing of the blind man in John 9. Pain is a creation of God and not necessarily the result of sin. It was created originally to protect us.

John Frame contributes to the topic of the origin of suffering in his great work on systematic theology. He also grounds the origin of suffering in the Fall. The result of the sin of Adam and Eve in the garden had personal as well as cosmic implications for all of creation.[94]

In their wonderfully helpful book, *Concise Reformed Dogmatics*, J. van Genderen and W. H. Velema write powerfully about the cause of suffering, evil, and pain. Sin has left wounds on creation. We can see that against the backdrop of a created world that God pronounced as very good (Genesis 1:31). The world as it is today does not reflect God's original creation. It groans under the weight of sin and evil (Romans 8:22). It waits for the anticipated liberation from sin and suffering just as humanity does. The authors write that sin is the great evil. Behind all questions of suffering is the world's guilt in sin. God has brought punishment upon all of His creation for the disobedience of Adam and Eve. Suffering and death are that judgment. The writers remind the reader that when we start from a position of guilt and sin, the real question is not why there is so much evil, suffering, and pain in the world but why God tolerates them in his long suffering. The new orthodoxy of a passible God, which is discussed in the chapter on sovereignty, starts with Auschwitz and the Holocaust, but Genderen and Velema prompt the discussion not to the twentieth-century horrors but back to the reality of Golgotha. The cross of Jesus is the only answer to sin and the suffering it has produced.[95]

As Philip Yancey said in one of his many books, "Giving a child a pair of ice skates knowing he may fall is different from knocking him down." God often uses pain and even suffering to accomplish his own good plan. We will look at that fact when we consider God's sovereignty and when we look at the cross of Christ. C. S. Lewis, in his book *The Problem of Pain*, reminds us that God often uses even suffering for our eternal good. He writes, "God whispers to us in our pleasures, speaks in our conscience, but shouts in our pains: it is His megaphone to rouse a deaf world."[96]

The Western world suffers the least and handles it the worst. We devise all sorts of drugs and other coping mechanisms to avoid suffering and pain. COVID-19 has shown us how fragile our society has become. In a way, it has balanced the playing field for all nations.

Perhaps one of the most helpful books to my ministry here in Louisville has been Diane Langberg's work, *Suffering and the Heart of God: How Trauma Destroys and Christ Restores*. In it, she examines how to do ministry in a Christian Community during traumatic times of suffering, as well as giving practical help to the counselor and counselee. She reminds the reader that sin has caused creation to be altered, but God, Himself, was not. Frequently, the suffering Christian mixes these up. The believer reasons from creation to God rather than from God to creation. It is a natural human reaction to ask why, but the folly of that question is that it has to be someone's fault. Yes, ultimately, God stands behind all suffering in some form, but such questions can be debilitating. The more personal the suffering is, the more likely we will struggle to handle it. Suffering is simply a way of life the Bible tells us, and it can attack anyone at any time unannounced. Health or wealth are never gods worthy of our adoration and worship. They can never be allowed to rule our lives. We are created for God's glory. Suffering is never our purpose in life.[97] Yet, unfortunately, so many people let their suffering define who they are in life. All that they do revolves around their trauma and not their real purpose in Christ.

So, we have seen that sin is the origin of suffering. Since the rebellion of Adam and Eve, devastation comes to every person's life at some point. Let me close with a couple of final thoughts. First, expectations play a big role in our suffering. We expect God to answer our prayers in the way we want Him to do it. Particularly in America, we expect God to shower us with blessings and to protect us from harm. When bad things happen, and we should say that suffering is bad, we claim that God is not fair. Christians need to be aware that their own personal expectations of God and His providence in their lives play a great role in whether they will flourish in suffering and grief. Expectations shape our ability to find hope and meaning in chaos. They often govern our reliance and growth in difficult circumstances.

Expectations can shape our mental attitudes and mindset in the midst of suffering. If we view suffering as an insurmountable mountain, we will never flourish and grow. We can feel overwhelmed, helpless, and alone. Conversely, if we believe God would never bring suffering into our lives, we can easily become discouraged and depressed. In contrast, if our expectations are grounded in the fact that God never leaves His children alone and that He governs all that happens, we can see these times as opportunities to learn to grow in our reliance on Him.

As we try to cope with times of suffering, if we see these challenges as unending and completely disruptive with only bad long-term consequences, we may turn to unhealthy coping strategies to deal with our troubles. These can lead to isolationism and unhealthy practices of addiction. But if we set our expectations in God's providence, mercy, and care, we will seek healthy ways of coping with the help of others. We will ground our expectations in a realistic understanding of our circumstances. We can adapt to our new circumstances by deepening our faith in Jesus Christ, knowing that these momentary troubles are preparing us for glory (2 Corinthians 4:17-18). Healthy expectations alone are not enough to flourish in suffering. They are, however, a necessary part of enduring suffering in Christ.

Second, we should note that all the other world religions and philosophies offer no hope in suffering. Atheism has a mechanistic universe where there is no god. Therefore, there is no standard of goodness outside the universe. Evolution and bad luck are what we experience. Each person decides good and evil for himself or herself in each situation. Because atheism rejects a higher power or a transcendent purpose, the atheist is left without any anchor to an ultimate reality or meaning. Therefore, suffering is purely random. The very existence of suffering has no explanation. Even though some atheists hold to moral opinions and judgments, in the context of suffering, they have no basis for judgment as to whether suffering is good or bad.[98]

Religious dualism is another view of suffering and God. There are many people who believe that God is less than all-powerful or less than omnipotent. They believe that God does not stand behind evil at all; it is always the fault of someone or something else. God simply cannot stop it. In the acclaimed book by Rabbi Harold Kushner, *When Bad Things Happen to Good People*, he believes that God could not prevent the death of Jesus. Neither God nor Satan is absolute in their power. The problem here is that this God brings no comfort. Who can hope in a god that is less than all-powerful, and who cannot control what happens in creation?

Others believe in a Deist God who is the creator but is never personal or immanent. This is the idea of the watchmaker who winds up the world and then lets it run out on its own merit. This god cannot bring any level of comfort or personal care. The deist believes in a universe that operates under the laws of nature, which are impersonal to human suffering. So, the chaos in life is just part of the random world, a natural consequence of life. Self-reliance is critical for the deist to survive suffering, and such self-reliance is always in opposition to the grace of God.

Then, there are many in the world who have a pantheistic worldview. These people believe that God and the world are one. There is no difference between the creator and creation. All is God. We see this in the Hindu, New Age, and other religions. This is "the force" of Star Wars. For the pantheist, all is divine. Therefore, the pantheist struggles to explain suffering and pain. How does moral responsibility or any definition of right and wrong get settled where everything is God? There is no place to draw near for comfort. If personal responsibility does not exist, it is difficult to work toward change. There is no court of appeal to go to for redress.

Finally, I would mention what has been called the free will defense of God. This argument says that if we are moral beings and are to be held accountable to God, we must be absolutely free. Therefore, God is not in control of evil and suffering. Suffering is simply random, with no purpose or meaning behind it.

When we say we believe in an all-powerful and all good God, we must also ask hard and difficult questions about evil and suffering; but only such a God can bring comfort and the promise of help in suffering. There is an answer to being content in our suffering. It only comes in the person and work of Jesus Christ. Christ alone brings us comfort and stability in turbulent times.

Perhaps we should ask the question, did God know that sin would enter the world? Did God plan for suffering to happen when sin happened? Did it surprise Him or catch Him off guard? These are the questions we will consider in the lessons ahead. Next, we will consider the Old Testament and how God somehow stands behind our suffering and pain. Is God truly sovereign?

CHAPTER FOUR

FOUNDATION STONE: SOVEREIGNTY

LESSON: GOD'S SOVEREIGNTY AND SUFFERING IN THE OLD TESTAMENT

In our last chapter, we looked at the origin of suffering and determined from Scripture that it comes from sin. We live in a fallen world, and all humanity, indeed all creation, is affected by the Fall. Sin pervades everything in the universe and so suffering is all around us. It comes into every person's life at some point. So, we know that suffering is the result of sin.

We also held up three critical statements. First — God is all-powerful. Second — He is all good. Finally, suffering and evil exist. Now, we hold these in tension because the Bible does. They are not contradictory, even though they may appear to be that way to some people. God is not the author of sin. He created us for love with free will, thus setting up the possibility of rebellion. That is exactly what Adam and Eve did in the garden; they rebelled against God.

In this chapter, we want to consider the sovereignty of

God and how that relates to suffering. We will begin to do that by looking at his sovereignty in suffering in the Old Testament. What exactly do we mean by God's sovereignty? Basically, it means that God is, well, God. James Boice defines it this way, "God is absolute in authority and rule over His creation. He is all-knowing, all-powerful, and absolutely free. He is supreme over all things." This is to say that nothing unforeseen or unplanned happens with God. There are no accidents, no surprises. R. C. Sproul's statement is: "There are no maverick molecules."

There are many solid books and articles on the Sovereignty of God. J. I. Packer's classic, *Knowing God*, deals with his sovereign care over his elect.[99] In A. W. Pink's *The Attributes of God*, the writer reminds the believer that no doctrine generates more comfort than God's sovereignty.[100] A.W. Tozer's two-volume work, which has the same title, has a very helpful chapter on God's sovereignty, where he writes that there are never any accidents with God.[101] David Powlison has also authored a book entitled *Suffering, God's Grace in Your Suffering*. It discusses God's work as a catalyst to reveal true faith and how God wants His children to trust in Him in the chaotic times of life.[102] Finally, in John Murray's short pamphlet, *Behind the Frowning Providence*, the author details his belief that God has for His children a connection to His glory through our suffering as He prepares us for eternal life with Him.[103]

A wonderful journal article by Sunday Bobai Agang entitled "Divine Sovereignty: The Challenge of Christians Coping with Suffering in the 21st Century." The author details God's sovereignty as it relates to how we handle suffering. In particular, the author brings his background with the suffering found in Nigeria to a very helpful article where he argues that with the loss of an understanding of the sovereignty of God, which he attributes to several events and shifts in the 21st Century, Christians have lost their ability to cope with suffering. Without the underpinning of this foundational truth, people do not know how to handle suffering.[104]

God's sovereignty is found throughout the Bible. We could start in Genesis 1:1, "In the beginning God created the heavens and the earth." He created it all out of nothing, so He is sovereign over it all. Proverbs 16:9 says, "In his heart a man plans his course, but the Lord determines his steps." Ephesians 1:11 says, "In him we were also chosen, having been predestined according to the plan of him who works out everything in conformity with the purpose of his will." Finally, Psalm 115:3 says, "Our God is in heaven; he does whatever pleases him." We could consider many more verses.

What I want us to think about is that perhaps intellectually, we all would assent to these verses and this doctrine of the sovereignty of God. From a distance, it looks reasonable and even helpful. But functionally, in your time of great pain and suffering, do you really believe it? Can you live it? When your doctor says you have cancer or when your child dies in a car wreck, or when your spouse has Alzheimer's disease. Can you worship God in His sovereignty then?

We learn what our relationship with God is like in the fire of suffering. Job certainly found this to be true. The Book of Job in the Old Testament has long been considered the Bible's book on suffering. As you may know, it centers on Job's character. There is this cosmic conversation between God and the Accuser in which Job is attacked by Satan with God's permission. As we read in the first session, Job loses all his children and his material wealth in one day. The depths of human despair and moral outrage are on display.

But the Book of Job is more about the integrity of God than the question of "Why" in suffering. Suffering is only the context for the discussion. Can God be trusted in times of unmerited pain and heartache? Job is a righteous man, yet he suffers greatly. How do we understand what God is doing? What becomes clear as you read the book is that God can and does use suffering for his purposes and is sovereign over it. The book is a rebuttal to Retribution Theology. That theology says that we suffer only as a result of some specific sin. Job's friends assume, incorrectly, that Job had committed some great atrocity and God was punishing him.

However, there are other great examples of suffering and God's sovereignty in the Old Testament. The Psalms of Lament are the largest category of Psalms in the Bible. A lament is simply a cry out to God for help in times of suffering and pain. Individual and Corporate Laments for the nation are found throughout the book. We may think of Psalm 13:1, where the psalmist says, "How long, O Lord?" We can consider Joseph or Jeremiah or Elijah or Daniel. In Daniel 4:35, we read that Nebuchadnezzar praises God and says, "All the peoples of the earth are regarded as nothing. He does as he pleases with the powers of heaven and the peoples of the earth. No one can hold back his hand or say to him, 'What have you done?'"

In the rest of this chapter, I want to talk about God's sovereignty in three areas — nature, nations, and individuals as it relates to suffering. The functional question we need to ask of God and his Word is simply this, "Does God ultimately stand behind my suffering?" Is my chaos and trauma simply a random act of nature? Does God even know or care? My friends, we must get this truth, this foundation stone, in place in our hearts and our minds to survive suffering with faith and hope.

There is a new telescope in orbit around Earth now — the Webb Space Telescope. With it, we can see into the far reaches of the universe; we now estimate that there are perhaps as many as 200 billion galaxies in the universe. That is not stars but collections of stars. Some individual galaxies have in themselves billions of stars. All that the Bible says about that in the creation story is that God made the stars also, and all of it reflects God's creative glory. But does God control our world? We have already said that creation is marred by sin, so does God control nature? We know that He sends a flood to destroy all the earth except for Noah and his family. What about all the suffering that comes from tornadoes, hurricanes, earthquakes, droughts, famines, and other natural disasters? Is God responsible for them? In the Book of Job, we know that God allows Satan to stretch out his hand and strike Job's surroundings; he just cannot take his life. Satan then uses lightning to kill off Job's animals, but even more tragically, he uses a windstorm to destroy the house where all his children are gathered, killing them all. Where is God in all of this? Is he ultimately in control or not? If he is really in control, can he be good in any sense?

The important point here is where do we place our eyes. Do we look at Satan's hateful and destructive hand or at God's sovereignty even over the horrors of nature? When thousands are killed on 9/11, or a tsunami washes away more thousands, can we still hold to God's providence and care? What about when COVID-19 kills millions? John Piper has written one of my favorite quotations, "If we spare God of the burden of his sovereignty, we lose our only hope."[105] God has to be sovereign even over tragedies because he is our only hope. The Bible is clear that the winds and waves, all of nature, obey His command. We could think of Jesus calming the storm in Mark 4 by simply saying to the wind, "Peace be still."

God is sovereign over the entire animal world as well. We see this in that He sent a fish to swallow Jonah or caused a plant to grow to give him shade outside Nineveh, and then He sent a worm to eat it, so it withers. He caused the ravens to bring Elijah meat and bread daily in the wilderness. The gnats in the plague of Egypt come and go at His bidding. This means that while Satan can and does use animals and plants to bring suffering, we can trust God that He holds the reins to it all. That means that the lions of the Roman Coliseum, the pit bull that attacks the child, or the COVID-19 virus that sickened and killed so many, casting our world into chaos, are all ultimately controlled by God Almighty. So, while Satan can bring suffering to the world through his use of animals, plants, and viruses because he is the prince of this world, God stands behind him, limiting his powers and reach.

God is also sovereign over nations. In John 17, Jesus says that God has given Him authority over all people. We can again turn to the Book of Job. The Chaldeans and Sabeans were both used to bring disaster onto Job. Think of all the Old Testament stories where God uses the nations of the earth to punish the Israelites for their disobedience. The Assyrians carry off the ten northern tribes. The Babylonians destroy Jerusalem and carry the people off for seventy years into exile. The Philistines harass God's children. Proverbs 21:1 says, "The King's heart is in the hand of the Lord; he directs it like a watercourse wherever he pleases." Colossians 1 says that all things, including all rulers and governments and authorities, are created by Him and for Him. Great suffering has come from nations. We can think of the Holocaust and the

Killing Fields, the human tragedy that comes from all the wars. Yet God is sovereign over even that. His sovereignty is our hope when the fog of life blinds us from seeing the work of his hand.

If God is sovereign over nature and nations in suffering, we can safely say He is also sovereign over individual lives. If you watch the news or read news online, you know that we live in a world dominated by evil and suffering. Random killings, drunk drivers, accidents on the road or in the air, disease, broken homes, mental illness, and abused children all show so clearly that we live in a sinful, fallen world. Missionaries die for their faith. People lose their jobs because they are Christian, or they are passed over for a promotion. The doctor tells you about your child's diagnosis. Your loved one is called to endure years of pain and suffering with some illness. Mental illness changes your loved one into a stranger. When suffering comes calling into our personal lives, that is when the doctrine of God's sovereignty becomes real. That is when our functional faith can cloud out our intellectual faith. Suffering reveals exactly where our relationship is with God. We are forced to live out what we really believe in the foundations of our hearts and minds.

The Bible is clear that God is sovereign over every

aspect of our lives. He knows the number of the hairs on your head. Even our time of death is set by Him in all eternity past. In his new book, *Seasons of Sorrow*, Tim Challies writes about his son's sudden and unexpected death at the age of twenty. He says, "And so I trust that Nick lived the number of years, days, hours, minutes, and seconds that were perfect for him. His life was not cut short, but he lived to the final moment of God's good plan. He was kept by God until he was ready to go and ready to be taken, ready to be gathered in. And then God called him home. In the wisdom of God, and according to the will of God, he died not a moment too late and not a moment too early." God is never surprised. He ordains whatsoever comes to pass. In the coming chapters, we will discuss the questions of purpose and meaning in suffering.

Now I want to make sure we understand God's sovereignty as it relates to humanity and our own actions. If God controls everything, does that mean that I am not responsible for my own actions? If God has ordained and planned everything, even down to using Satan and suffering, do I have any responsibility for how I live? The short answer is yes — you are responsible for what you do and how you act.

While God's sovereignty in the actions of humanity is sure, nowhere does the Bible tell us that we are not responsible for our own sinfulness just because God is somehow behind our actions. The story of Joseph in the Book of Genesis points out this fact in vivid detail. You may remember the story where Joseph is a younger brother of Jacob's sons. They despise him because he is their father's favorite. So, they sell him into slavery, and Joseph ends up in Egypt as a slave of Potiphar. While God blesses everything Joseph puts his hand to, Potiphar's wife claims he tried to assault her, and he ends up in prison. Eventually, Joseph was raised to become second in command of all of Egypt during a great famine. Finally, his brothers are driven to come to Egypt for food; although they do not recognize him, they come before Joseph. Eventually, he reveals himself to them, and all of his family moves to Egypt. But when their father dies, they worry about Joseph harming them. But Joseph says in Genesis 50:20, "You intended to harm me, but God intended it for good." His brothers are guilty of selling him into slavery, but God was not just contingent in the situation; he is accomplishing his good plan. God is at work even in the middle of evil and pain.

Perhaps the best place we see man's responsibility for his own sinfulness held up with God's sovereignty is in the sermon of Peter at Pentecost as we find it in Acts 2:23. "This man (Jesus) was handed to you by God's set purpose and foreknowledge; and you, with the help of wicked men, put him to death by nailing him to the cross." You see, the Romans and Jews were responsible for killing Christ, yet it was the plan of God all along to accomplish the work of salvation. The death of Jesus Christ on the cross is an unimaginable horror and great evil, yet God had planned it all along for his glory and our good salvation. Yes, we have free will to do what we want. But that free will is never absolute power. We cannot confound the purposes of God.

The last major point I want to make as we finish up our very brief look at God's sovereignty is to ask the question, does God, who is completely sovereign over everything, suffer when we suffer? After all, this is the critical question, isn't it? If God controls everything in all creation, even somehow standing behind our suffering, does He feel anything when we have pain and trauma? We know that God does not change. Immutability is an attribute of His. Jesus is the same yesterday, today, and tomorrow, the writer of Hebrews says. In Malachi 3:6, we read, "For I the Lord do not change."

No study of God's sovereignty and suffering would be

complete without examining the doctrine of God's impassibility. The impassibility of God has been historically taught by the church and confirmed by the Westminster Confession of Faith, describing God as "a most pure spirit, invisible, without body, parts, or passions."[106] Since the second century, it has been held by church fathers.[107] A basic definition of the doctrine is that God cannot be acted on by anything outside his own nature, and, therefore, is incapable of suffering. It is against his very nature to do so.[108]

Amos Oei believes that in the twentieth century, the impassibility of God has fallen out of vogue as a classic dogma. The world, even of theology, has sought to lift up feelings and discard difficult truths. Much of the criticism of this doctrine is highlighted in Jürgen Moltmann's book, *The Crucified God*. His effort is to cast this doctrine aside for a more appealing God to a society that over-emphasizes emotions. If God can suffer, then He can feel with humanity. If He cannot suffer, He is "poorer than any man."[109] John Stott, in his classic work, *The Cross of Christ*, seems to affirm Moltmann's understanding of a God who suffers.[110] Kenneth Cauthen notes that Warren McWilliams, in his book *Passion of God: Divine Suffering in Contemporary Protestant Theology*, and Douglas John Hall, in his work *God and Human Suffering: An*

Exercise in the Theology of the Cross, have written extensively about this movement. McWilliams gives a running list of theologians who have jettisoned impassibility, such as Moltmann, Jung Lee, Geddes McGregor, and James Cone. These authors believe that God must suffer if He is to be able to bring any comfort.[111]

The rejection of God's impassibility has grown out of a belief that Greek philosophy had influenced the early church Fathers to such an extent as to warp their understanding of what the Bible actually says. Many theologians in the last century have begun to view God as a vulnerable deity. Kevin DeYoung details four reasons for this change in the classical doctrine. First, a suffering God is the only way to understand suffering and develop a solid theodicy. Second, if God is truly love, He must be able to enter into our pain and suffering. Third, the Bible must be taken at face value, and the anthropomorphic language used in it cannot diminish God. Finally, Jesus Christ, as the fullness of God in human form, suffered on the cross. His suffering demonstrates for us the true nature of God's suffering. Kevin DeYoung notes in the writing of Richard Rice that the cross of Jesus is the suffering of God Himself.[112] But DeYoung is quick to point out the error of a passible God, and he holds fast, it appears, to the classic understanding that God cannot suffer.[113]

This new orthodoxy means that God is subject to emotional change and is vulnerable to powers outside Himself.[114] It strikes to the very heart of the doctrine of God's immutability. If God is truly changeless, as Scripture affirms, then He cannot be acted on by anything in creation (James 1:17; Psalm 102:25-27; Malachi 3:6). He must always remain faithful and morally constant. He can never waiver in His word or character. So, how does the reader understand the multitude of passages in the Bible that at least seem to point to the fact that God has emotions and feels emotions? We read that He rejoices (Isaiah 62:5), grieves (Psalm 78:40; Ephesians 4:30), burns with wrath (Exodus 32:10), pities (Psalm 103:13), and loves (Isaiah 54:8; Psalm 105:17). How do we affirm the Westminster Confession and these verses? To be realistic, the supporting verse for this part of the confession (Acts 14:15) is not helpful at all.

Fortunately for this author, John Frame, J. I. Packer, and others bring clarity and understanding to the doctrine of impassibility that is faithful first and foremost to the biblical record but also to the teaching of the early church Fathers. Frame reminds us that the Bible speaks, in many places, of what is described as God's emotions, such as compassion, tender mercy, patience, delight, pleasure, pity, love, wrath, and jealousy. While these emotions seem to support passivity and change, God responds differently to different events. His emotions are more evaluations of what happens. He shows empathy (Hebrews 4:15). He goes on to write that Christ suffers on the cross in His human nature, but it is not the nature that suffers but the person. God the Father never suffers in the same way as God the Son suffers. When God grieves or suffers, He never suffers loss. He concludes that God's suffering love in Christ never dilutes His immutability.[115]

Amos Oei grounds his argument for the impassibility of God in His immutability. God cannot be changed, and therefore, He can never be affected by anyone or anything in creation. He writes that even Tertullian believed that God has emotions, but His emotions are of a divine manner and radically different from our human emotions. Impassibility does not mean being inactive or uninterested in creation. God possesses His emotions in the greatest possible power and intensity. He reminds his readers that Calvin understood that all of God's revelation in the Bible must, of necessity, be anthropomorphic because God, in His immensity and holiness, must speak to us in baby talk, such as when he says he repents (Genesis 6:6). He speaks to us in language we are capable of understanding in our limited capacity and fallenness. He condescends to accommodate us in His revelation of Himself. Otherwise, we would never be able to understand our covenant relationship with Him. Oei's contribution to this topic is very helpful. He writes that we should always let our understanding of God shape our suffering and never let our suffering shape our understanding of God. God understands and overcomes; He empathizes with us and is compassionate to us. Finally, Oei writes that God's emotions are analogous to our emotions but never equivalent. Our emotions are analogous to God's emotions only because we are created in His image. His emotions are beyond our emotions.[116]

Derek Rishmawy brings clarity to some of the terms in the defense of impassibility when he reminds his readers that the early Fathers distinguished between passions and affections. Affections were defined as controlled emotions that are subject to the will. The biblical descriptions of God's emotions must be something more than mere anthropomorphic language. Rishmawy argues that God has what Kevin Vanhoozer calls "cognitive emotions." God never has the rush of emotions brought on by outside influences. His affections are judgments or attitudes toward His creation. Rishmawy gets the closest to that argument of J. I. Packer when he states that God's feelings in relationship to His creation is not something He must passively suffer but that which He actively chooses to endure in His sovereign will.[117]

Can God relate to me in my tears? Does He suffer when I suffer, or is He simply the cosmic watchmaker who winds up His world and walks away? As I read Scripture, I would say yes, God does suffer when we suffer, but NOT in the same way we suffer. What do I mean? God cannot be acted on by outside influences. Nothing can change God. Yet we are created in His image with emotions and the capacity for love and, therefore, the capacity for pain and suffering. So, I believe two things. First, there is no doubt that Jesus Christ suffered on the cross. He is our suffering servant, and we will discuss that more in our next section. However, God must, in some way, experience our heartache with us even as He is refining us for His glory. He must have something akin to an emotional life. He has feelings in some way that we cannot completely grasp. God suffers with us because He sovereignly wills to suffer with us. He chooses to do so. What great comfort then His sovereignty is!

After reading all of these writers and seeing the various arguments for impassibility, I understand that intellectually, they all held together in support of both God's changelessness and His impassibility. But for this writer, the argument that God, in and of Himself, cannot in some way relate to me in my suffering, enter my suffering, feel the pain of loss and grief beyond just Christ on the cross left a gap in my personal theodicy. Suffering is not simply intellectual; it is real and existential.

As a cancer survivor and as a pastor, my heart hurt for the couple that I met for the first time to begin pre-marriage counseling. I had just asked the young man to tell me about his relationship with Jesus Christ when he broke down uncontrollably and began to sob openly. As the story unfolded, it seemed that the young man had surgery for testicular cancer back in April and was told that the surgeon thought it was all gone. They began to plan their wedding in earnest. Then, as we were to begin our counseling sessions that week, they found out his cancer had spread to his lungs and lymph nodes. In their pain and suffering, what did God have to say to them in that moment? Did He empathize with them? Was the doctrine of impassibility so important that even in God's immanence, He did not feel anything for this young man and his bride-to-be?

J. I. Packer brings this writer to a better and clearer understanding. He writes that there is absolutely something in God that corresponds to our emotional life. It would be horrid if God had no feelings. Scripture says that He does feel. Packer reminds all of us that when God feels, even when God suffers, He does so out of his sovereign will. When the Bible says He feels pain, suffering, and grief, it is never in an involuntary way as a victim of the outside world but only in a manner to which He has chosen to do. He is never the victim of man. Grief and suffering are part of the eternal plan of salvation and history. He planned to experience distress and has budgeted for that. Behind the human story of change is the fixed plan of God. Christ, in suffering on the cross, then becomes the supreme sympathizer. There is the willed and planned suffering of God as He empathizes with us in our pain. However, as previously stated, God's suffering is analogous to our suffering but not identical. Our description of God's suffering is only to accommodate us and to reveal His eternal love. It is never that God experiences any type of loss in His suffering but is afflicted by His eternal will. He is never a victim. He sovereignly chooses to accept all of our pain and grief as part of His providential care for His beloved children.[118] As another person has said, the cancer patient does not want God to experience cancer with him but wants a physician who understands the pain and suffering and can bring a cure and relieve the pain and suffering. God does that in the person of Jesus Christ. The Bible never presents God as far from us in our time of need.

D. A. Carson would seem to echo support of Packer. In fact, in his book *How Long, O Lord?* He really asks only one simple question, "Does God suffer?" His conclusion is that God does absolutely suffer, but not in a way that is identical to our suffering. Those who have stood firm on the weaker definition of impassibility, namely that God cannot suffer, have gone so far as to make Jesus Christ out as "schizophrenic." The Bible clearly speaks of a God who is both completely sovereign and transcendent and one who is emotional and personally interacts in a relationship with His children. To claim that all of the passages in Scripture that show Jesus as having feelings and emotions cannot be written off simply as anthropomorphic. They have to refer to something; they have to mean something. Again, Carson notes it is not a suffering God that suffers identically to the way humans suffer, but one who is analogous to our suffering in some way. The anthropomorphic language must be a metaphor to refer to something in God. He loves and has personal relationships with His elect. The cross is where the Christian finds God suffering in human terms.[119]

The takeaway from this chapter is that God is absolutely and completely sovereign. He ordains everything that happens for His glory. That does not mean that God is the author of evil and sin, but He allows or permits such things to happen in accordance with His goodwill. He stands asymmetrically behind good and evil. We must always, always hold to the truth that God is all-powerful or sovereign, and yet He is always all good. The Bible proclaims these two truths over and over. We must view His sovereignty through the lens of His perfect goodness, righteousness, and holiness. He suffers with us, particularly in the person of Jesus Christ, and it is to Jesus that we will next turn our attention.

No matter how much we learn about God and His sovereignty, we must always remember that we are finite, and He is infinite. Scripture tells us that His ways are not our ways nor His thoughts our thoughts. (Isaiah 55:8-9). The Book of Job again helps us here when we read in chapter 26, "These are but the outer fringes of his works, how faint the whisper we hear of him! Who can understand the thunder of his power." As F. W. Boreham writes in his essay, "The Whisper of God," we are only children picking up shells on the shores of eternity.

CHAPTER FIVE

FOUNDATION STONE: SHEPHERD

LESSON: THE SUFFERING SERVANT AND THE CROSS

We are now at our halfway point in building our foundational truth for surviving and, indeed, thriving in times of suffering, pain, chaos, and trauma. We have seen that sin is the source of suffering. When Adam and Eve rebelled against God in the Garden of Eden, all creation, including all humanity, was marred and fractured by sin. The penalty for sin was spiritual death and a fallen creation where suffering is now woven into the great fabric of all that there is. Our first foundation stone is Source, which states that sin is the source of all suffering.

We also know that God is sovereign. That He somehow stands behind even sin and suffering for His own glory. In fact, the point of all creation is for God to show the glory of His grace to mankind even in sin and suffering. God is all good and all-powerful. He ordains everything that is in accordance with his perfect will and holiness. Our second foundation stone to endure suffering is Sovereignty!

If we are alienated from God by sin, dead in our sins and trespassed as the Bible says, then what hope do we have in our sin and suffering? It is one thing to know that God is perfect and holy, and therefore, controls everything and yet is not the author of sin. But is there any hope? The prophet Isaiah wrote 700 years before the birth of Jesus Christ, and yet, he foresaw the one who would come, the Suffering Servant. Here are his words from Isaiah 53:2-9:

> He grew up before him like a tender shoot, and like a root out of dry ground.
> He had no beauty or majesty to attract us to him, nothing in his appearance that we should desire him.
> He was despised and rejected by men, a man of sorrows, and familiar with suffering.
> Like one from whom men hide their faces he was despised, and we esteemed him not.
> Surely he took up our infirmities and carried our sorrows, yet we considered him stricken by him, and afflicted.
> But he was pierced for our transgressions, he was crushed for our iniquities;
> the punishment that brought us peace was upon him, and by his wounds we are healed.
> We all, like sheep, have gone astray, each of us has turned to our own way;
> and the Lord has laid on him the iniquity of us all.
> He was oppressed and afflicted, yet he did not

open his mouth;
he was led like a lamb to the slaughter, and as a
sheep before her shearers is silent,
so he did not open his mouth.
By oppression and judgment, he was taken away.
And who can speak of his descendants?
For he was cut off from the land of the living; for
the transgression of my people he was stricken.
He was assigned a grave with the wicked, and
with the rich in his death,
though he had done no violence, nor was any
deceit in his mouth.

Perhaps we may have heard of this passage because we know that Jesus Christ is this Suffering Servant. This is the one who carried our sorrows on the cross. My friends, to properly understand how we deal with and live through suffering, we must make sure that we have a proper understanding of what Jesus Christ did for us on the cross. We must view our suffering through the lens of his suffering on the cross.

What exactly happens at the cross? Why is this the pivotal moment in all of human history? The Bible is very clear. God entered time and space in the person of Jesus Christ. He alone has lived a perfect life. He never sinned; He never rebelled against His heavenly father. But He entered time and space because of the plan of God. Before creation, God knew sin would happen and planned to use it to show off the glory of his grace. Jesus came to pay for my sin and your sin on the cross. He willingly took your guilt and mine onto himself and willingly credited to us his perfect righteousness so that we who call on him as Lord and Savior might live forever. The Apostle Peter gives us these words in 1 Peter 2:21-24:

> To this you were called, because Christ suffered for you, leaving you an example, that you should follow in his steps.

> "He committed no sin, and no deceit was found in his mouth."

> When they hurled their insults at him, he did not retaliate; when he suffered, he made no threats. Instead, he entrusted himself to him who judges justly. He himself bore our sins in his body on the tree, so that we might die to sins and live for righteousness; by his wounds you have been healed.

Christ came to suffer and die for all who believe in Him. He willingly endured all the punishment and wrath for your sin and mine. God poured out our judgment onto Christ because the Father loves His followers that much. Jesus, in the garden before His death, is in agony of heart. He prayed for another way. He struggled to face His calling to suffer. Yet God had planned this from all eternity for the salvation of many. Christ, in His humanity, suffered and died on the cross. Then on the third day, by the power of the Holy Spirit, the father raised Jesus back to life. In the resurrection, Jesus conquered death, suffering, and pain. As we just read, He is our example of suffering. This is why Jesus alone is worthy of trusting in our times of pain and trouble. He has suffered for us. He knows what it is to feel the anguish of heartbreak, fear, and trauma. The cross redefines everything because God in Christ willingly and purposefully suffers for us. It is on the cross that He deals with suffering, pain, selfishness, and hurt.

John MacArthur's book, *The Power of Suffering*, details his argument that suffering plays an important role in the life of the Christian as it draws the person closer to Christ, our Suffering Servant. It is Christ who provides us with the perfect example of suffering. He answers the ultimate questions of suffering. In his powerful chapter, "The Silence of the Lamb," MacArthur details many of the New Testament passages that speak to Christ as our Suffering Lord (Galatians 6:14; 1 Peter 2:20-23; Hebrews 2:10, 5:8-9). Jesus is our sinless and humble sufferer and our model for us to follow in our lives as we suffer.[120]

We might well ask how Jesus does this for us. As Jesus prays in the Garden of Gethsemane for not His will but God's will to be done, He shows us the path of humility (Matthew 26:39). He willingly sets aside the human desire not to suffer and takes up the mantle of our pain and suffering for us. While we will suffer in various ways in this life, He takes on the ultimate suffering for us. Secondly, He shows and models great love for the elect in dying for those called by God. If Christ has loved us so much that He would take our worst suffering, it can only mean that He abides with us in our earthly suffering and pain.

Martyn Lloyd-Jones writes, in his book entitled *The Cross*, that the cross of Christ teaches us how to suffer. In expounding on 1 Peter 2:18-25, he says that Christ has endured all suffering for us on the cross and can, therefore, lead us and comfort us in our suffering. We are simply called to follow Christ in His footsteps.[121]

In Peter Kreeft's book, *Making Sense Out of Suffering*, the writer talks about the Incarnation as the greatest event in all of human history, where God came to earth to take on human nature to seek a personal relationship with God's children. Because of this glorious fact, Christ enters into our suffering with us. His presence with us and the assurance of his love for us are all we need. He is the "man of sorrows, and familiar with suffering" (Isaiah 53:3). Kreeft rightly believes that the cross is the context for all our suffering. It explains suffering and gives it real meaning. On the cross, Jesus accomplishes three important things. First, He weeps and suffers. Second, He transforms the meaning of suffering as part of the plan of redemption. Third, He transforms death into the birth pains of true, eternal life.[122]

Our redemption comes then in Christ's death on the cross. What sin had so completely broken, Christ restored on the cross. He endured it all. The great English pastor, John Stott, says that Christ is God's personal and loving solidarity with us in our pain. After all, who could trust a God who never knew suffering and pain?

We are also called to enter into His sufferings with Him. Later in his letter, the Apostle tells us in 1 Peter 4:12-16:

> Dear friends, do not be surprised at the painful trial you are suffering, as though something strange were happening to you. But rejoice that you participate in the sufferings of Christ, so that you may be overjoyed when his glory is revealed. If you are insulted because of the name of Christ, you are blessed, for the Spirit of glory and of God rests on you. If you suffer, it should not be as a murderer or thief or any other kind of criminal, or even as a meddler. However, if you suffer as a Christian, do not be ashamed, but praise God that you bear that name.

This is why Jesus tells us that if we are to be His disciples, we are to take up our cross daily and follow Him! The cross of Christ as the Suffering Servant is the marvel of our forgiveness. God forgives us because He punished his only Son. The beauty of forgiveness, which is the result of His suffering on the cross, should never dim in our eyes. Even if our suffering is the result of our own sinfulness, we find the glory of grace in the forgiveness that comes to us in the cross. I am reminded of the poem about an elementary school teacher:

> He came to my desk with a quivering lip,
> The lesson was done.
> "Have you a new sheet for me, dear teacher,
> I've spoiled this one."
> I took his sheet, all soiled and blotted
> And gave him a new one all unspotted.
> And into his tired heart I cried,
> Do better now, my child.
> I went to the throne with a trembling heart,
> The day was done.
> "Have you a new day for me, dear Master?
> I've spoiled this one."
> He took my day, all soiled and blotted
> And gave me a new one all unspotted.
> And into my tired heart he cried,
> "Do better now, my child."[123]

It is on the cross of Christ that the justice and love of God meet. The penalty of sin, which the Bible tells us is death, is paid for there. It is Christ who suffers for us in love. "God made him who had no sin to be sin for us, so that in him we might become the righteousness of God" (2 Corinthians 5:21). The cross shows us how personal this God we love really is. He is never far off in our time of need but intimately with us and for us.

Don Carson puts it this way, "In the darkest night of the soul, Christians have something that Job never knew. We know Christ crucified. Christians have learned that when there seems no other evidence of God's love, they cannot escape the cross."[124] Hear what He says when we cannot see for the tears of our suffering, when we cannot hear over the cry of our pain, Christ is always there. He knows because He lived it. Every aspect of Christ's saving work is accomplished in suffering.

Jeremiah Denton was the highest-ranking POW in the Vietnam war. After weeks of beatings and starvation, he sat in the dirt contemplating his own devastating and seemingly hopeless situation. He thought of Mary as she stared at Christ on the cross. He would later write these words while a prisoner of war during Easter in 1969. In part it reads,

> Her face showed grief but not despair,
> Her head though bowed, had faith to spare.
> And even now she could suppose,
> Her thorns would somehow yield a rose.

Her life with him was full of signs,
That God writes straight with crooked lines.
Dark clouds can hide the rising sun,
And all seem lost when all be won.

When Christ calls us to take up our cross daily and follow Him, He is calling us to die to ourselves, our pride, our wills, and our worldly passions so that we might live for Him. Part of that living for Him is also suffering for Him. Discipleship is dying to things not worthy of hanging onto to allow Christ to be our all in all.

Why? Why are we called to suffer with Him and for Him? The Book of James gives us the answer in 1:12, "Blessed is the man who perseveres under trial, because when he has stood the test, he will receive the crown of life, that God has promised to those who love him." You see, my dear friends, ultimately, Jesus Christ saves us from the worst of suffering — eternity in hell. He endured the cross for the joy set before Him — and we have that same joy set before us.

So how does all this talk of Christ and His suffering functionally work its way out in our daily lives as we suffer? After all, not all of our suffering is directly tied to living for Christ. Lung cancer strikes when you have never smoked. The child dies without anything we can point to for a cause. The mind deteriorates simply from old age, and lifelong partners become strangers. How does Christ's suffering on the cross also help us in these types of crises of life? To be honest, even if I had sinned, when devastating news comes and suffering follows, ultimately, it is wonderful that my sins are forgiven. But how do I endure with hope that pain I have? How does Christ carry me when my child is suffering, or some chronic disease will cause me to live in severe pain for many years?

The answer is that the Suffering Servant is also the Good Shepherd. The 23rd Psalm reads, "The Lord is my shepherd; I shall not be in want. He makes me lie down in green pastures; he leads me beside quiet waters." It goes on to say that He leads us even through the valley of the shadow of death without fear! When we think about how Christ meets us in our suffering, an Old Testament story from the Book of Daniel comes to mind. You may remember that Daniel is in Babylon under the rule of King Nebuchadnezzar. Daniel's three friends, Shadrach, Meshach, and Abednego refuse to bow down and worship the golden statue that the King has made. As punishment, they are thrown into the fiery furnace heated seven times hotter than usual. They are bound and thrown in, yet the king sees not three men but four walking around in the furnace. These men are unbound now, unharmed by the fire, and the fourth one looks "like a son of the gods"

(Daniel 3:25). When the three are brought out, there is not even a hint of smoke on their clothing.

That is an illustration of how Christ meets us in our time of need. He stands with us in our pain and suffering. He grieves with us as we grieve. He holds us as we die and carries us to glory! This is not to mitigate or deny our troubles in this world. Jesus told us in John 16 that we would have trouble in this world but to take heart because he had overcome the world. He says in Matthew's Gospel, "Come to me all who are weak and heavy burdened, and I will give you rest." We may not always know the "Why" of our suffering, but we can rest in Christ. We can rest in the knowledge that he knows every moment of our pain, and the Savior of your soul is willing to suffer with you. Our souls will always find rest in Jesus, our Good Shepherd.

There is an eternal dimension to our suffering that Jesus wants us to see. We might call this understanding of suffering, the view from eternity. In eternity, there will be no more pain, crying, or death. There will be no more suffering. We will enjoy an eternity of worship in whole, resurrected bodies. There is a beautiful passage in 2 Corinthians 4:16-18 where Paul speaks about our suffering in this world and the gift that Christ gives us at the cross. He writes:

> Therefore we do not lose heart. Though outwardly we are wasting away, yet inwardly we are being renewed day by day. For our light and momentary troubles are achieving for us an eternal glory that far outweighs them all. So, we fix our eyes not on what is seen, but on what is unseen. For what is seen is temporary, but what is unseen is eternal.

Jesus Christ, who is the same yesterday, today, and tomorrow, will lead you through whatever valley of suffering may come your way. He will lead you! That means there is a purpose, a meaning to His direction. We may not know the answer to the "Why" question, but we can endure suffering with the knowledge that our Savior leads us with a purpose in all that He does. Our hope is that God is being somehow glorified in my circumstances.

Let me close with this powerful statement from Don Carson in his book *How Long, O Lord?* He writes:

> Christians will take refuge from their suffering not in bitterness, self-pity, resentment against God, or in trite clichés, but in endurance, perseverance, and faith in God who has suffered, who has fought with evil and triumphed, and whose power and goodness ensure that faith resting in him is never finally disappointed.[125]

It is the idea of significance and purpose that we will turn in our next chapter.

CHAPTER SIX

FOUNDATION STONE: SIGNIFICANCE

LESSON: THE PURPOSE OF SUFFERING

So far, we have laid three of the stones into our foundation for enduring suffering with hope and meaning. We have seen that the Source of suffering is sin. Humanity and all creation are distorted by sin. The world is not the way God originally created it. Suffering might come from my own sin or the sin of others, or even the work of Satan, but it all originates in sin. Our next stone was Sovereignty. God ordains everything that happens, yet He is not the author of evil. He is all good and all-powerful, and yet evil exists. The Bible holds these three truths in tension. The next stone we placed in our foundation was Shepherd. Jesus Christ is not only the Suffering Servant who died for us on the cross and, therefore, knows our pain and sorrows, but He is also our Good Shepherd who leads us through the dark valleys of suffering in our lives. Hand in hand, we walk with him as he guides and comforts us.

Now, as we come to our fourth stone for the foundation, this one may be the one you have been waiting on because we will address the question of meaning in suffering. Is there a Significance to our pain, grief, and heartache? Can we functionally believe, actually believe in the routines of our everyday lives, that God works all things for the good of those who believe, who are called according to his purpose (Romans 8:28)? In other words, do we truly believe that in the worst circumstances of life that God is sovereign and at work for our good and His glory? This is where the rubber hits the road. This is where our faith meets the realities of living in a world where suffering is a part of the fabric of life. The Bible handles suffering and grief and pain and chaos with openness and honesty. It never belittles our pain, yet it provides comfort and meaning. God never wastes anything He does.

People struggle when they suffer. They can suffer physically, emotionally, spiritually, intellectually, or all of them at once. "Why" is most often the question. Why is this happening to me or my loved one? Why does God not love me anymore? Where is God now? Most Christians do not want someone to suffer the same issue as them but someone who is able to empathize with them. They want to know, above all else, if there is any kind of reason for why they are going through all of the chaos in their lives. Is there a purpose to it all?

We all should expect pain and struggles, grief and suffering in our lives. The Bible is very clear about that fact. We live in a fallen world. But suffering never catches God off guard. He is never surprised by suffering. As believers, in Jesus Christ as Lord and Savior, we need to desperately learn to suffer well. To do that, we must learn that, for Christians, there is always a purpose in suffering. However, our expectations, especially in America, are that we should not have pain and struggles. We don't deserve to suffer. We do everything we can to avoid it.

After 9/11, there was a PBS Special entitled "Faith and Doubt at Ground Zero" that included some people's comments about God in the aftermath of the tragedy. The quotations ranged from "I've decided that God is a barbarian" to "All of God's attributes were swept away that day." Another said, "I'm losing my respect for God." Finally, someone gave these sad words. "I know I need to forgive God, but I just can't." These types of comments grow from a culture that never expects suffering and where God's sovereignty has been abandoned. Our expectation is that God will only bring a bed of roses without the thorns.

In all honesty, though, even if we believe God is at work, suffering is hard to endure, and the longer it lasts, the harder it is to be grace-filled and trusting. Questions of "Why?" always arise. We are made with intelligence and want to know the reasons behind things. It is part of our nature. When suffering makes no sense to us, these questions are never far from our minds. It can be so sudden and senseless, so devastating and final. Suffering never seems good in any way. It is the unwanted thief who steals our faulty belief that we are in control of our lives. Many people do not think deeply about suffering and faith, but I am convinced that if we want to remain faithful and trusting in God, we all need to do just that when the waters of life are calm. We must build the foundation of our faith on solid ground before the untimely storms of suffering arrive in life.

So, back to our question — is there meaning and purpose in our suffering? The Bible says YES! Will God always make known to you His reasons and specific plan for your suffering? — NO. We do not know the secret things of God, but His Word, the Bible, does give us promises to hold on to during these turbulent times for comfort. If we say that God has no part in our pain, then we truly would have no hope. In his article for World magazine entitled "Governor of All,' John Piper writes, "If we relieve God of the burden of His providence (sovereignty), we lose our only hope."

A god who has no part in our suffering, who can be bullied aside by fate or the work of the devil, can never bring any comfort. A god who does not care what happens to you offers no solution. But that is not the God of the Bible. The God we find there is the one about whom Nebuchadnezzar says in Daniel 4:34-35:

> At the end of that time, I, Nebuchadnezzar, raised my eyes toward heaven, and my sanity was restored. Then I praised the Most High; I honored and glorified him who lives forever.
> His dominion is an eternal dominion;
>   his kingdom endures from generation to generation.
> All the peoples of the earth
>   are regarded as nothing.
> He does as he pleases
>   with the powers of heaven
>   and the peoples of the earth.
> No one can hold back his hand
>   or say to him: "What have you done?"

Our world is fallen, and sin has marred it, yet God is still absolutely good, righteous, holy, and in control of every single atom. Behind all of our suffering is God's divine hand. A God who cares, loves, is longsuffering, merciful, and nurturing to His children. He is never absent, vengeful, or hostile toward us. All that He does is for His glory and our ultimate good. Somehow, He stands behind the traumas of our lives and the evil of this world and brings good from it. His promises are always sure and firm.

But God rarely answers our questions of "Why me?" or "Why now?" or "Why did this have to happen?" Scripture is full of reasons and ways God uses suffering for His perfect plan. After studying suffering and pain for more than twenty years now and looking at what the Bible has to say about it, I have found that the better question is, "To what end?" What are you wanting me to do or learn? How can I be refined in all this suffering? My prayer has evolved to, "Lord, don't let me waste my opportunity to grow in my faith during my suffering. Teach me what I need to learn to be more Christ-like through this situation."

There are many different ways we could talk about God's purposes in suffering, just as there are many different types of suffering. Pain and trauma can happen to us physically, mentally, and spiritually. We can suffer as we care for someone else who is suffering. Suffering comes when we love. Circumstances can lead us to struggle as one might do in poverty. Others suffer mightily for their faith in Christ. Persecution and hardships from the secular world are part of the Christian life. But no matter the category we label a particular kind of suffering, the question we need to ask is, what is God doing in it? If we know He is sovereign and at work even in the midst of this terrible situation, what is He trying to accomplish?

Various scholars, writers, and commentators have tried to categorize most suffering into various general categories. Joni Eareckson Tada and Steven Estes list thirty-six purposes or categories for suffering. They offer detailed explanations of each. Each reason listed is followed by verses from Scripture to support their perspective. The authors suggest that to understand what God is doing in our afflictions is to understand his Word. Some of the listed reasons could easily be combined into a simpler list, but the strength of their work is in their references to and grounding in the Bible.[126]

Tremper Longman III and John Walton put forth five categories. These include physical suffering, which is pain that comes from injury or chronic disease. Psychological suffering comes from the loss of a loved one or some other type of grief. Circumstantial suffering can arise from living with mental illness or acquired diseases from poor decisions. Surrogate suffering is when you live with a suffering loved one, and you suffer with and for them. Finally, they list systemic suffering, which happens when one lives in poverty or is under a repressive government. These categories add the idea of suffering associated with sins someone commits and God's punishment for such sins. All of these categories are grouped under the general headings of "sin" or "creation incomplete."[127]

Layton Talbert gives at least four categories of suffering. Persecution is suffering for the sake of Jesus Christ. We find this type of suffering throughout the Bible (Acts 7:54-60; 1 Peter 4:14). Punishment is the next category he gives the reader. This suffering, delivered by mankind, is deserved and just (1 Peter 4:15). Next, Talbert says chastisement is deserved suffering from God (Lamentations 3:1). Finally, he lists affliction as undeserved suffering that is not understood and has no basis in a specific sin but is permitted by God. This is the suffering that is most often considered in the Book of Job.[128]

Eric Ortlund advocates three categories of suffering. First, he writes that suffering may be categorized as a result of sin on the individual's part, which can have a direct one-for-one correlation without a necessary timeframe. Second, suffering could be God at work in our lives, bringing us into greater conformity with our Savior. Last, Ortlund lists a type of suffering where God is simply giving us more of himself. This category is also similar to the suffering of Job. God brings suffering so that we can hold on to God for God's sake alone.[129]

J. I. Packer sees the wisdom of God in all suffering. He writes that all circumstances of our lives are ordered by God's wisdom for either our personal growth in holiness and sanctification or for the fulfillment of God's ordained ministry in the life of his people.[130] There is often an increased sense of appreciation for the insights God gives us from these seasons of suffering, no matter how painful the circumstances or how many unanswered questions.[131] John Calvin suggests that suffering brings men to repentance and weans us from too tight a hold on the things of this world. Suffering can and should move us to prayer. The pain and trouble of this world are God's voice and His hand of providence, which helps us to know God and ourselves more fully.[132]

In John Murray's delightful, helpful, and readable booklet, *Behind the Frowning Providence*, he reminds his reader that the Bible clearly tells all God's children that suffering is a normal part of the Christian life. In Hebrews 11, we find a summary of the suffering of many faithful in the Old Testament. In the New Testament, we have our greatest example of how to live in and through suffering in the person of Jesus Christ. Murray also inserts chapter 5, paragraph 5 of the Westminster Confession of Faith, in which it is written that God, in His providence, often uses suffering for the good of His children. He lists six ways in which God uses suffering and fuses it with purpose. First, sufferings are to try us or to build our faith. Second, Murray says that sufferings are to expose our sin. Third, suffering builds character. Fourth, suffering brings us to know God better. Fifth, suffering produces fruit in our lives and prepares us for service. Sixth, suffering leads us to make God our all and to prepare us for glory. The author's wisdom and many quotations from the Puritans bolstered each of these reasons. He closes his writing with comfort in times of chaos. He quotes Charles H. Spurgeon, who wrote, "When we cannot trace God's hand, we can trust God's heart."[133]

Paul David Tripp writes about suffering out of his own personal experience with life-threatening pain and sickness. He cries out from his own hospital bed, "Why." Suffering can appear so suddenly and without warning. It can seem so purposeless. It robs the sufferer of the "illusion of control." He writes that the Bible says there is always a purpose in suffering. The chaos of the moment may blind us to that purpose, but the Bible is clear in its accretion that there is purpose. Tripp grounds his writing on the sovereignty of God. The very fact that God providentially controls all that is and happens in life tells us that there is a plan and purpose (Daniel 4:34-35). Following loosely after John Murray, Tripp gives four reasons or purposes in the plan of God for suffering, each supported by Scripture. First, he writes that we suffer because we live in a fallen world (2 Corinthians 4:7-10). Second, we suffer because God uses it to produce good in us. It exposes our self-reliance, self-righteousness, and our idols (James 1:24). Third, suffering prepares us for how God will use us (2 Corinthians 1:3-9). Fourth, suffering teaches us that this world is not our final home (2 Corinthians 4:16-5:5).[134]

Sunday Bobai Agang writes powerfully about suffering in Nigeria in the 21st century. The writer says that the attitudes toward sovereignty have changed significantly over the years. Including a quotation in the article from A. W. Pink where he writes that today, mentioning God's sovereignty "is to speak an unknown tongue," Agang reminds the reader that understanding God's sovereignty in suffering is the key to coping and surviving existentially. We are fellow heirs with Christ (Romans 8:17). Suffering has the ability to build character, cleanse our heart, grow our empathy towards others, and make the sufferer more tenderhearted. All of this is to grow our faith and to make us more Christ-like. Agang believes that human suffering has a much deeper purpose in the grand plan of God. We are called to do ministry in the context of pain and suffering. As Dietrich Bonhoeffer said, when Christ calls us to follow Him, He calls us to die with Him.[135]

In the end, suffering is part of God's design and providence, His good sovereignty. We trust Him when we cannot understand the question "Why me?" James Dobson puts it well when he writes: "We serve this Lord not because He dances to our tune, but because we trust His preeminence in our lives. Ultimately, He must be and will be the determiner of what is in our best interest. We can't see the future. We don't know His plan. We perceive only the small picture, and not even that very clearly."[136] The Apostle Paul tells us that while we see now darkly, one day we will see clearly as we come into His eternal kingdom and enjoy the splendor of his mercy and grace unclouded by sin and fallenness (1 Corinthians 13:12).

Every book on suffering at some point has a chapter or section about God's purposes in suffering. They all boil down to a few basic ones in one way or another. So, while you may not know exactly what God is weaving in your life, you can know He is at work making a beautiful tapestry of your life as part of His grand kingdom. Let me suggest three ways that God uses suffering in the believer's life. I say the believer's life because God uses suffering very differently in the non-believer's life. The fruit of suffering is very distinctive for the Christian.

First, God uses suffering to convict us of our own sin. Sometimes, there is unconfessed sin in our lives, and God brings adversity into our routines so that we will see our sin, repent, and return to Him. We see that in Hebrews 12:5-7:

> And have you forgotten that word of encouragement that addresses you as sons: "My son, do not make light of the Lord's discipline, and do not lose heart when he rebukes you, because the Lord disciplines those he loves, and he punishes everyone he accepts as a son." Endure hardship as discipline; God is treating you as sons. For what son is not disciplined by his father?

God disciplines us for our own good. A simple example of this might be a person who gets a speeding ticket because he drives much faster than the speed limit. Another verse we could consider is Psalm 107:17, in which the psalmist tells us that some suffer because of their sin.

The second general category for the purposes of God in hardship is personal growth and transformation. In other words, God uses anguish and difficulty to shape us and mold us to become more like Jesus Christ. The Bible says we are to share in Christ's suffering. God often brings it into our lives for our own spiritual growth. This is the category of discipleship that the Bible speaks most often about in terms of suffering. There are many verses we could reference here, but let me relate to a couple.

Romans 5:3-4, "Not only so, but we also rejoice in our sufferings, because we know that suffering produces perseverance; perseverance, character; and character, hope. And hope does not disappoint us, because God's love has been poured out his love into our hearts by the Holy Spirit, whom he has been given to us."

James 1:2-4, "Consider it pure joy, my brothers, whenever you face trials of many kinds, because you know that the testing of your faith develops perseverance. Perseverance must finish its work so that you may be mature and complete, not lacking anything."

Finally, Philippians 3:10-11, "I want to know Christ and the power of his resurrection and the fellowship of sharing in his sufferings, becoming like him in his death, and so, somehow, attaining to the resurrection from the dead."

These and many other verses all point to how God uses misery in our lives to shape and humble us. As one insightful writer has said, God cares more for our character than our comforts. Godliness is the goal of all believers in this world. God uses suffering to make us conform to His image. There is an anonymous poem that speaks so boldly to this truth.

> When God wants to drill a man
> And thrill a man
> And skill a man,
> When God wants to mold a man
> To play the noblest part;
> When He yearns with all His heart
> To create so great and bold a man
> That all the world shall be amazed,
> Watch His methods, watch His ways!
> How He ruthlessly perfects
> Whom He royally elects!
> How He hammers him and hurts him,
> And with mighty blows converts him
> Into trial shapes of clay which
> Only God understands;
> While his tortured heart is crying
> And he lifts beseeching hands!
> How He bends but never breaks
> When his good He undertakes;
> How He uses whom He chooses
> And with every purpose fuses him;
> By every act induces him
> To try His splendour out,
> God knows what He›s about!
>   (Author Unknown)

Suffering in the hands of a great and mighty God is a powerful tool to shape our lives. We do not rejoice because we suffer, but we rejoice in our suffering because God is at work. He loves us more than we could ever love ourselves. As Paul David Tripp tells us, God is producing in you what you would never be able to produce on your own. The terrible and tragic things we endure are tools of a very good thing God is doing in our lives. This is a critical lesson for our foundation. The bad, evil, and painful things we endure are being used by the Grand Weaver to make you, and perhaps others who suffer alongside you, into the people he has called you to be. We may hate it at the time and rail against God in our chaos. We may see the evil in our circumstances and scream about it. We may, in fact, see nothing in it that could ever in any way possible be labeled "good." And yet, our sovereign God is at work somehow.

Suffering has a way of exposing our frailties and cracks in our faith. It reveals our personal idols because we long for what is taken away that we secretly worship in our hearts. Our distress destroys our reliance on self and exposes to us and those around us our self-righteousness. The anger, doubt, impatience, and demanding nature that comes out during suffering was in our hearts all along. Our misery simply exposes it more clearly. Suffering is designed by God so that we can hold things in this world with an open hand and worship the only real source of comfort — our Savior, Jesus Christ.

Let me add, before we move to our last category, that as God transforms us through adversity, he is not only making us more Christ-like, but he is also preparing us for a lifestyle of ministry in this world. In 2 Corinthians 1:3-9, Paul tells us that God brings us comfort in our suffering so that we can comfort others. I have seen this firsthand in my own life and in others. The parents who lose a child are later able to minister to other families in their tragedy of such a loss. The cancer survivor speaks more boldly into the life of another in treatment because you have been there. Those who have walked their grief path are better at helping people in fresh grief. The results of suffering should never be an inward focus but an outward reach to help others in their time of need. As He trains us for ministry, persecution may come our way. The Bible has many stories of God's faithful suffering for their faith. The blood of the martyrs waters the soil in which the Kingdom of God grows best.

We have seen that God uses pain and grief to convict us of our own sinfulness. Second, we talked at length about how God uses our times of heartache to shape and mold us into His image and prepare us for ministry as a lifestyle. Finally, we need to see that God uses suffering to remind us that this world is not our final home. This life and world are not all that there is. To be honest, it is not even close to the best that there is. Yet, we live as if it is. We hold tight to the material things of this life as if when its gone, there is nothing left. Yet suffering and sin are not the way God first created the world, and it will not be our eternal home.

As I said earlier, God uses our pain to often pry open our hands from the death grip we have on things here in this world to kill the idols that hold our hearts bound to this world. God uses our hardship to teach us that there is something far, far better than this world for those who love Jesus. Paul writes out of his own suffering with these beautiful words in 2 Corinthians 4:16-5:8:

> Therefore we do not lose heart. Though outwardly we are wasting away, yet inwardly we are being renewed day by day. For our light and momentary troubles are achieving for us an eternal glory that far outweighs them all. So we fix our eyes not on what is seen, but on what is unseen. For what is seen is temporary, but what is unseen is eternal. Now we know that if the earthly tent we live in is destroyed, we have a building from God, an eternal house in heaven, not built by human hand. Meanwhile we groan, longing to be clothed with our heavenly dwelling, because when we are clothed, we will not be found naked. For while we are in this tent, we groan and are burdened, because we do not wish to be unclothed but to be

clothed with our heavenly dwelling, so that what is mortal may be swallowed up by life. Now it is God who has made us for this very purpose and has given us the Spirit as a deposit, guaranteeing what is to come. Therefore, we are always confident and know that as long as we are at home in the body we are away from the Lord. We live by faith, not by sight. We are confident, I say, and would prefer to be away from the body and at home with the Lord.

That is a beautiful perspective and faith in God. My prayer for all of us is that we would have the depth of faith to trust in God's holy work even when we don't understand and cannot see a way forward through the fog of our pain-induced tears.

CHAPTER SEVEN

FOUNDATION STONE: SURETY

LESSON: ABANDONED BY GOD, A PRACTICAL LOOK AT LEARNING TO TRUST CHRIST IN SUFFERING

Well, we have finally come to the last building block for our foundation to endure suffering with faith and meaning. This chapter will be a bit different from the others in that we will cover a variety of topics, and I'll include some practical help. We have seen that the source of suffering is sin. God's sovereignty, however, stands above and behind every detail of life. He alone is all-powerful and always good in every way. Jesus Christ relates to us in our suffering in that he is not only the Suffering Servant, but he also leads us through life as the Good Shepherd. He cares for us. Finally, we learned that a Christian's suffering has true meaning and significance, no matter what the cause. God is always at work in some way in our suffering.

We now turn to the foundational stone of Surety. One definition of surety is certainty or grounds for confidence.

As we have seen, God's sovereignty is the basis of our sure and certain hope. In Jesus's death, we are united to Him in His suffering as Christ leads us through adverse times. The Holy Spirit is the one who applies all of this to our situations and brings the comfort of Christ. 2 Corinthians 1:22 says that God has set His seal of ownership on us and put His Spirit in our hearts as a deposit, guaranteeing what is to come. For the believers in Jesus Christ, we know that this world is not all there is and that in eternity, we will live without pain and suffering. It is out of this surety that God calls us to live in hope and to be a comfort to others in their times of adversity, grief, and struggle.

Heaven is real, and we will live there forever with all God's children. It is our greatest reality. The surety we hold fast to in suffering is that God is holding us, Jesus is suffering with us, and the Holy Spirit will carry us in Christ to our eternal life of peace and joy beyond anything we can truly comprehend here in this life. COVID-19 may have shaken your faith in God; maybe it was because you lost a loved one or the economic traumas it brought, or the isolation we all endured. The one thing we did not see with the coronavirus was the turning to God as we had seen after 9/11. Most studies show that COVID-19 did not have much influence on faith in one way or another. But personal suffering can wreck our faith, no matter the cause. So, what are some helpful things we can do in our times of adversity? We want to look at practical helps both for the sufferer and for the one called to bring comfort and support. Out of the surety we have in Jesus Christ, we can do these things.

The first area of practicality I want to mention is prayer. Unfortunately, when we meet someone in need, most of the time, we say one of two things. First, we often say, "What can I do for you besides pray?" Or we say, "I'll pray for you," but we never do. Prayer is a great tool for us to use in our times of suffering and pain. Paul writes in Philippians 4:6-7, "Do not be anxious about anything, but in everything, by prayer and petition, with thanksgiving, present your request to God. And the peace of God, which transcends all understanding, will guard your hearts and your minds in Christ Jesus." These are such powerful verses, and we don't have time to dig into their depth. But we can see we are called to pray. Jesus in the Garden of Gethsemane prayed for another way other than his suffering to come. Yet, he was primarily pray-ing for God's will to be done. But notice in all Christ's prayers that He is submitting his expectations to God's will. Paul, when he prayed to be relieved of the thorn in his flesh, recognized that God, in not removing it, was using it for his own good. God's grace was sufficient in Paul's weakness.

We should pray for relief and healing in our times of crisis. The Psalms are full of laments for relief from suffering. In Psalm 13, David cries out three times, "How Long, O Lord?" Yet it ends with rejoicing as the psalmist comes back to the fact that God is always good and always in control. So, we see that we should pray for relief in our own suffering and for the relief in the suffering of others. But always with the ultimate goal, as Jim Boice reminded us, that God would be glorified in whatever happens. We pray, expecting God's will to be done, not our own personal desires.

Remember these five truths in our prayer lives. 1 — God's sovereignty assures us that the circumstances of life are not out of control. Nothing happens outside his perfect will. 2 — God's scale of time and our scale can be very different. We live in an instantaneous society, but that is not how God works. His timing is always perfect. 3 — For God, who wills and ordains everything that happens, there are no surprises. So, when disaster strikes unexpectedly, God is not caught off guard. 4 — God is a God of details. The little things are important to Him as well, so pray about them, too. 5 — God is a God who is intimate and responsive. He answers prayers in his way and timing. He cares for you and is at work in you. Pray for him to mold you as he wants. Prayer is designed in part to bring peace to us as we lay out petitions before God Almighty.

I have always been struck with the beauty of a prayer penned by Blaise Pascal, who lived in the 1600's and laid the groundwork for the computers we use today. A great believer in Jesus Christ, he wrote:

> I ask you neither for health nor for sickness, for life nor for death; but that you may dispose of my health and my sickness, my life and my death, for your glory.
> . . . You alone know what is expedient for me; you are the sovereign master; do with me according to your will. Give to me, or take from me, only conform my will to yours. I know but one thing, Lord, that it is good to follow you and bad to offend you. Apart from that, I know not what is good or bad in anything. I know not what is most profitable to me, health or sickness, wealth or poverty, nor anything else in this world. That discernment is beyond the power of men or angels, and is hidden among the secrets of your Providence, which I adore, but do not seek to fathom.

That is a prayer for God's will and glory!

Many books are available for practical help when we feel abandoned by God. Paul David Tripp's book entitled

Suffering, is a wonderfully helpful and pastoral book based on his own life story of suffering and the doctrines that have supported his walk with Christ over these many years. He reminds his readers that suffering is truly spiritual warfare and wallowing in self-pity is no solution. We are made for life with others in community. We were never made for outright independence from others. Everyone needs help and comfort at some point. He uses 2 Corinthians 1:8-11, in which Paul is dependent on God and others for his survival. When we join with others in our grief and suffering, the point of such community is not to share the various details of our suffering but rather to talk with others about how we are struggling in our pain. The help here comes from expressing honestly what you are going through. Suffering has a way of stripping us of the illusion of control and independence. In his chapter on companionship in suffering, Tripp writes of seven important points the sufferer needs to remember.

1 — Don't suffer in isolation. There is nothing heroic or helpful or noble about bearing your pain and grief alone. We were made for community, and the church is our community of faith to help surround us in our time of great need. Others can often make the invisible grace of God, visible to us. Fellow Christians are "God's instruments of grace" for you. They may say the wrong thing or

ask the untimely question, but we should never suffer in isolation.

2 — Be honest in your communication. Honesty in communicating with others about how you are struggling spiritually is always helpful. Those who come alongside you do not need to hear all of your complaints but do need to hear your honest assessment of your heart and soul. This is not to say be a complainer — that will chase people away. But be honest in your physical, mental, and spiritual battles. Others will come alongside you to fight with you. Community cannot help with what they do not know. Now, I know there are some people who refuse to be open and honest with others out of a fear of being vulnerable or seeming like they are just complaining. We need to be open and honest. Being open with close friends in Christ can help us share our burdens.

3 — Let others interrupt you. Let people in. No one talks to you more than you do. Tripp argues that we should allow others in to help us with our blind spots in how we understand our suffering. We can struggle to tell ourselves what we really need to hear. Others can bring comfort and insights that we would never say to ourselves. He writes, "God puts others in our lives to interrupt ourselves with things we would never tell ourselves."

4 — Admit your weakness. God is never honored when we publicly fake what is privately untrue. Saying you are fine when you are not is never ever helpful to you or the body of Christ. We don't open up to everyone, but we all need some folks we can be honest with. Be open and honest about your weaknesses. Acting as if we are handling everything well when we are falling apart inside dishonors God and keeps others from offering the help we so desperately need.

5 — Seek wise counsel. If you are in need, seek out the best counsel you can find from spiritually mature people for your spiritual battles and the best in their field for other needs. Suffering causes us to not think clearly or to know what is best. Shock, grief, fear, and anger can cloud our minds. If you are struggling through grief, never make big decisions quickly or in the immediate days after your loss. Suffering causes us to not think clearly or rationally. We should never make decisions alone.

6 — Finally, remember that your suffering does not belong to you. It ultimately belongs to God. 2 Corinthians 1:3-9 tells us this fact. God is at work in and through your life but also in the lives of others around you in ways you will never see. Tripp says one of the miracles of grace is that your suffering is being used by God to mold and

shape not only your character but the character of others around you. Suffering makes us uniquely qualified to sympathize with and help others in their adversities. Every sufferer should keep in mind that the comfort that comes in community works both ways. Others bring comfort to you, but God also uses you to minister to others.[137] I know this has been very true in my life.

One final note from Tripp's book on suffering is to remind the reader that suffering is never ultimate, but God is. God controls our eternity. The hardships of suffering do not define who we are; only God does that. The comfort that comes from God's mercy and grace can never be taken away from the Christian because believers are secure in Christ.[138] Suffering in isolation is never good because suffering should never define you. But many of us cannot make solid decisions about what to do in times of real sadness, crisis, sickness, and death.

I also found the work of Jerry K. Robbins, "A Pastoral Approach to Evil," to be a rich resource for a theological and practical approach to the problem of evil and how we are to bring comfort to others. He writes about what he calls "companionable care." Believers should always be offering care to others. Sufferers should never suffer in isolation. Such care confirms to sufferers that their illness or suffering does not define who they are. It challenges the thought that evil rules by showing there is a power stronger than evil itself, the love of God as shown through his children. Just showing up and being present is very affirming. Silence is a form of communication when we sit and abide with a sufferer.[139]

David Giese's article, "Trusting God When Your Boat is Sinking," reveals practical advice for times of chaos from Mark's Gospel. When the storms of life blow in abruptly, the believer needs to always remember that God is still in control with all his amazing attributes, and very importantly, He always cares.[140]

I don't know of another author who has written more clearly or practically on what we should do to bring comfort to those in suffering than Nancy Guthrie. She and her husband lost two babies to the same disease. She knows heartache, pain, and suffering.

Many of these thoughts are from her several books. Specifically, her book, *What Grieving People Wish You Knew*, is such a jewel in teaching how we can administer care and comfort and what is actually not helpful and potentially harmful. The power of presence in time of suffering is so valuable.[141]

In conversations, let the sufferer take the lead. One of the greatest lessons from the Book of Job is when his friends arrive and sit in silence with him for seven days before they say anything. Silence is a form of communication. Listen more than you talk or be okay with sitting in silence. Presence is a powerful tool. Simply showing up and not being scared to be quiet is really helpful to those in need. When you show up, be present and do. Don't wait to be asked. When we asked, most people said, "No, I'm fine." Bring a hot meal, if appropriate, stay and eat, particularly with a person who has lost a spouse. Cut the grass, clean the house, go to the grocery store, clean up the yard. Do something; don't just ask if there is anything you can do.

Don't assume their emotions, and don't compare their situation to yours. It is not about you. Don't say, "I know how you feel." Grief and loss in suffering are unique to each person. Don't be quick to talk about your own trauma unless invited by questions from the one you are trying to comfort. Don't offer Bible verses in an effort to fix their pain. Knowing Romans 8:28 as a foundation for your faith is one thing; quoting it to someone who has just lost a loved one is the wrong thing to do. If you want to offer the great comfort of God's word, weave it into a note to the person in sympathizing with them. You don't have to answer every question; offer every solution. Simply be with the person. You can't fix the person so that they are no longer suffering. Only Christ can bring true peace.

Don't tell someone in need what to do. Don't say you need to eat something, or you need to go to bed. Do say things like, "I'm so sorry for your loss," or "I really miss" and use their name. Don't try to minimize grief; recognize suffering for what it is — the loss of something we love. Don't recoil from tears and crying. We are called to weep with those who weep and rejoice with those who rejoice. Don't be curious and ask questions. Don't be afraid to use the loved one's name in a death situation. If there is a GriefShare program nearby, offer it or offer to go with them. Finally, don't presume God's purposes with unhelpful statements. Never say things like, "Well, God needed another angel." Not only is that unbiblical, but it also offers no comfort. We are far greater than angels, for we are created in the image of God.

Some positive things beyond showing up and being present are asking about a favorite memory of the loved one or story. Take the children for a play date. When someone is sick, helping them with daily responsibilities is a huge help. Write notes. I still have every card I was sent when I had cancer. Leave messages that you were praying for them if they don't answer the phone. Being active for others is helpful to those in need.

There are a few helpful devotions out there for people in grief and suffering if you are asked. Resist the urge, however, to drop off books that address their issue. But when asked, provide proven resources. One book to mention would be one from Joni Eareckson Tada, in which she writes twenty-five helpful devotions on suffering based on various Bible verses and includes a hymn with each devotion. Not only are the hymns grand, but the pictures are beautiful. Her words come from the heart of a life-long sufferer. I found this book so helpful for personal worship time in the middle of suffering.[142]

I want to close our time out with a brief word about contentment in suffering. We will remember from our last lesson that our lives were never meant to be comfortable, secure, and happy in this world. Our lives are meant ultimately for God's glory alone. It is man's chief end as the catechism says. We are training for eternity here. As one author said, this world is a lousy home but a great gymnasium. We are called to be content even in suffering, pain, loss, and chaos. We should never be content with this world, but we should always be content in this world.

We can do that by resting in God's will and trusting in his perfect wisdom and purposes.

> Paul tells us this in Philippians 4:11-13:
> I am not saying this because I am in need, for I have learned to be content whatever the circumstances. I know what it is to be in need, and I know what it is to have plenty. I have learned the secret of being content in any and every situation, whether well fed or hungry, whether living in plenty or in want. I can do everything through him who gives me strength.

Paul had learned to be content no matter what his circumstances were. Spiritual contentment is always grounded in and based on our relationship with Jesus Christ. It is never found in the materialism of this world or the circumstances in which we find ourselves.

How do we get to where Paul was when he wrote that he had learned to be content? We can do this by placing these five foundation stones of faith under our lives as we grow our relationship with Jesus. By building our faith on the truths we have talked about here, we build contentment. The source of all suffering is sin. God is sovereign over everything, being all good and all-powerful and yet, never the author of evil , but he uses and controls it for his glory and our good. Jesus Christ, our Lord and Savior, knows suffering and suffers with you in your time of need. He leads us through the dark valley for his glory and our eternal good. There is significance in our pain, fear, and trauma. God is at work molding you in some way for His kingdom now and equipping you for eternal life with Him. Finally, we can have the surety of faith and trust when our circumstances do not make sense and what is happening to us cannot be said to be good in any way.

Taken all together, these stones allow our lives to withstand anything this world can throw at us, any pain and interruption life may bring. We can stand firm because we have built our house of faith on the solid rocks of God's eternal, foundational truths found in His Word.

Amen.

Appendix One

COVID-19 and Issues of Trust

Practically as we now live in a post-Christian world and in the grip of a worldwide pandemic that just will not go away, several works by Carey Nieuwhof and the Pew Research Center (PRC) will bring us full circle to how we should trust God when the foundations have been destroyed. Has COVID-19 changed our trust in God? A brief overview of what has been written in light of the pandemic is helpful to our look at suffering. Certainly, the pandemic has heightened our world's suffering.

In his article, "5 Reasons You Still Feel Disoriented, Dissatisfied, and Depleted," written in 2022, Carey Nieuwhof says that COVID-19 has certainly had an impact on clergy and the church. More than fifty percent of pastors he surveyed felt worse now than they did a year ago. The old normal is no more. Pastors are grieving and trying to process all of the changes and the loss of consistency. Their emotions have not yet re-aligned with the newness of it all. COVID-19 has split the country and the church with deep divides. Finding a new normal for ministry is still a work in process.[143]

But what about the communities into which pastors minister? Have the attitudes of those in the pews changed toward God? Has the pandemic eroded their trust in God? These are important questions for the issue of suffering. The PRC has done several studies on these very issues.

A PRC survey of adults in the United States in March 2020 showed that ninety percent reported that Coronavirus had impacted their lives. The overwhelming majority felt uncomfortable even going outside their homes. More than half, fifty-five percent, had prayed for an end to the pandemic. Of that number, eighty-two percent were evangelical protestants. Fifty-nine percent attended religious services in person less often, and online watching of services increased by fifty-seven percent. Four in ten replaced in-person attendance with virtual attendance. Thirty-three percent said that they or someone in their home had lost a job or had to take less pay. Many intimately knew the tragedy of the changes brought on by the pandemic.[144]

The PRC also did a worldwide survey in the fall of 2020 looking at the strength of religious faith in fourteen advanced, economically developed countries. Twenty-eight percent of the American response reported that their faith had actually increased because of the pandemic. That figure was the largest of any of the developed nations surveyed. Interestingly, thirty-five percent of Americans surveyed believed the pandemic brought with it lessons from God. Because of the secularization of Europe, it was not surprising that only a small minority believed that religion was even important in their lives. However, while the number of those who claim no religious affiliation grows in America and the percentage of people attending church shrinks, most surveyed reported that religion is important in their lives. Generally considering the results of the survey, in developed economies, not much has been changed by the pandemic in terms of religious faith. Few differences came to light from the survey, with women being more religious than men in Christian-majority countries.[145]

In November of 2021, PRC found that few Americans blame God for the outbreak of COVID-19. Many said their faith had not been jeopardized or eroded. However, a close look at the data revealed that most of the responders held an underlying belief that tragedies and other bad things happen randomly. When asked to explain suffering, eighty-six percent said that they agreed or somewhat agreed that bad things just happen, and they are random. Seventy-one percent agreed or somewhat agreed that suffering is a consequence of people's own actions. Yet sixty-one percent said that they believed suffering was not in vain. In the same survey of those who said that they believed in God or a higher power, eighty percent said that suffering comes from people and not from God. Seventy percent say mankind is free to act against God's will and plan. In the end, only fifteen percent of believers said that the existence of suffering had changed their view of God.[146]

Finally, PRC published a survey in October 2021 as worship services began to open back up to congregants. This survey found that there was no clear evidence that places of worship had a positive or negative impact on Americans' response to the pandemic. Seventy-three percent of evangelical protestants say clergy had not spoken to the issue of vaccines. Sixty-one percent said they have at least a "fair amount" of confidence in their religious leader's guidance about vaccines. Of these respondents, they said they were more willing to trust their religious leaders over the state and elected officials about vaccines. Only primary care doctors scored higher in trust on vaccines. What is clear from this survey is that the majority did not think that the church had much impact at all on how the United States responded to the pandemic. Some, twenty-five percent, even believed the church had harmed the response.[147]

All the PRC results seem to show there has been little change in faith due to the pandemic. This may mean that faith plays a relatively small role in life with little understanding of the sovereignty of God. Yet, of those surveyed, a majority seem to trust their clergy. There was no evidence through this research that pointed to a decrease in faith in the midst of this tragedy, the ensuing chaos, suffering, and death. The next avenue of research the author wanted to follow was the psychological impact of COVID-19 on mental health and how views of God and suffering impacted those who held religious faith.

In an article published in January 2021, Elizabeth Hall et al. examined "sanctification theory." For the purposes of their article, they defined sanctification as "the process by which people appraise life as having divine character and significance." In their study, seventy-nine percent of people who see God as active in suffering had positive outcomes from suffering. Christianity can provide a positive form of coping during periods of suffering and pain. They believe the results of their studies show that in Christianity, suffering can be redeemed to accomplish God's purposes and to shape individuals to become more Christ-like. The authors of the article write that they identified several ways this happens. Suffering is permitted by God's will (Job 1:12, 26). Suffering is for God's purposes (Romans 5:3-5; James 1:2-4). Finally, they found suffering can connect the sufferer to God (Philippians 3:10-11). Within their study, they developed the Christian Sanctification Scale, which was used to measure those with a theistic tradition. It was supported by the Views of Suffering Scale (VOSS) rating used in the same studies. These scaled ratings all pointed to a sense of meaning in suffering when the sufferer has a corresponding dynamic view of God as part of their personal faith and doctrine. These ratings can then accurately reflect the fact that the person finds meaning in suffering.[148]

In May 2022, academic publisher MDPI put out a fascinating article from five researchers concerning religious views on suffering during COVID-19. The study looked at individual theodicies at the beginning of the pandemic and the outcomes of that religiousness and psychological well-being. In other words, the research looked at how participants dealt or coped with the increased stress and suffering that came with the pandemic. It has been well established that disruptions to the normal routine of life (suffering) seem to increase stress and anxiety. COVID-19 brought its own unique stresses, such as social distancing and isolation. Other research projects, according to this study, have found a positive association between commitment to one's faith and greater personal satisfaction, and better overall well-being in life. Religion can be important to making sense of suffering. Positive mental health outcomes are linked to faith.[149]

The study referenced recent research by Wilt et al. and Park et al. that showed that those who viewed God as being more active and involved in suffering reported more satisfaction with their own faith. Those who view God as more passive in their suffering had a less fulfilling engagement with their beliefs. It appears from the research that one's personal theodicy can have an important impact on adapting to the pandemic. This research study also used the VOSS that was developed in 2012 by Hale-Smith et al. as a measure of God's role in suffering. The scale measures, on a one to six scale, responses between God and suffering in ten subscale units consisting of three statements each. Statements ranged from God using suffering to build character to God being unable to stop suffering. In their research, they found that those who hold to retribution theology were more depressed, more anxious about life, and were in more spiritual distress. Those who believed in a God who sovereignly controls everything found they had fewer worries and fewer mental health issues. The VOSS was helpful in connecting the view of God to the effects of suffering. Again, the research showed that those who view God as active in their suffering were more committed to their faith and had the lowest level of anxiety and better dealt with stress. The God who suffers with the sufferer brought the best results in terms of mental health.[150] It was the VOSS that helped me create my own survey for my participants in the five lectures.

In a short article published by the American Psychological Association, Bryan Goodman writes that researchers and those in clinical practices are discovering that religion and faith are more important to coping with suffering and chaos in people's lives than they realized. Research points to the fact that such people can see life's tragedies through the lens of hope, thereby engendering a sense of connectedness. It is the rituals of religious life that connect people together and to God. He does warn, however, that for those who believe in a retribution theodicy, religion can do more harm than good.[151]

From a psychology and mental health standpoint, the evidence is powerfully supportive of a theistic worldview and of a sovereign God who is active in our lives. Those who hold to such a view and find their relationship with God important will weather times of suffering much better than those who do not hold an active view of God.

While theology is the queen of the sciences, more

interest is being generated now that suffering and science have met in the COVID-19 world. Rian Venter writes that he believes more research should be done on the relationship between science and theology. This trend seems to be centered in South Africa. In particular, in the pandemic age, does virology impact the doctrine of creation? How does the study of philosophy and pandemics interact with human life and belief in God?[152] These are some of the new questions on the horizon in the COVID-19 age.

Lea De Backer echoes these same thoughts when she writes about mental health in South Africa during COVID-19 lockdowns. Her questions revolve around how virology impacts mental health and what role religion has in that mix. She says there is no doubt that the isolationism forced on society during the first months of the pandemic has increased addiction and mental health issues. She claims that interpersonal neurobiology is real, and science is just now telling us what the Bible has said all along. We are made for social interaction; we are social creatures made for relationships.[153]

In his article for TIME, N. T. Wright criticizes the extreme views that theologians have taken on the pandemic. Whether it is a punishment from God, a warning to repent, or just a need to find some excuse, Wright finds them all unhelpful. Wright is agnostic toward the crisis, believing that the response from the church should be to lament in the biblical tradition. While biblical laments in the Psalms often end in praise, he calls for the church to lament because God also laments. Christians, even in isolation, are a "small shrine where the presence of God can dwell."[154] He expounds these thoughts even more in his earlier book, *God and the Pandemic*, where he writes that Christians must be the "signs" of John's Gospel, where believers show with action the love of Christ. This means ministering into the pandemic. The clergy should be allowed to pray over the dying. Churches should volunteer in shelters and food banks when others are unwilling to venture out.[155]

One of this author's favorite writers has given us a small book on God and COVID-19. John Lennox writes that everyone must deal with the pandemic in three different areas of life: intellectually, emotionally, and spiritually. He reminds his readers that all pain is not bad; it can warn of danger and is part of physical development. Pain contributes to our character development. Lennox references C. S. Lewis when he notes that our worldview affects our attitudes in suffering. A powerful point in his book is that if God is removed from the equation of pain and suffering, it still leaves the sufferer with pain and suffering. Nothing is gained.[156] He concludes his argument that our ultimate hope in times of tragedy is in the cross of Jesus Christ. Christ can be trusted even when we do not have all or any of the answers. He alone brings peace.[157]

Endnotes

Chapter 1

1 Paul David Tripp, *Suffering: Gospel Hope When Life Doesn't Make Sense* (Wheaton: Crossway, 2018), 20-21.

2 All references and quotations from Scripture are from the New International Version (1984) unless noted otherwise.

3 D. A. Carson, *How Long, O Lord?: Reflections on Suffering and Evil* (Grand Rapids: Baker Books, 1990), 20.

4 John R. Stott, *The Cross of Christ*, 20th anniversary ed. (Downers Grove: InterVarsity Press, 2006), 301.

5 Tripp, 23.

6 Lee Strobel, *The Case for Faith: A Journalist Investigates the Toughest Questions to Christianity* (Grand Rapids: Zondervan Publishing House, 2000), 28.

7 C. S. Lewis, *A Grief Observed* (New York: HarperCollins Publishers, 1996), 17-18.

8 Elie Wiesel, *Night* (New York: Hill and Wang, 2006), 67.

9 Steven Davis, ed. *Encountering Evil: Live Options in Theodicy*, new ed. (Louisville: Westminster John Knox Press, 2001), 22.

10 James Emery White, *Christianity For People Who Aren't Christians: Uncommon Answers to Common Questions* (Grand Rapids: Baker Books, 2019), 45-54.

11 R.J. Gore. "The Problem of Pain." accessed February 3, 2020, https://drive.google.com/drive/folders/1OKmsX8R8gmT8QO1cg-expPOwmdjvin1S.

12 Diane Langberg, *Suffering and the Heart of God: How Trauma Destroys and Christ Restores* (Greensboro: New Growth Press, 2015), 104-106.

13 Eric Ortlund, "Five Truths for Sufferers from the Book of Job," *Themelios* 40,2 (Aug 2015): 254.

https://web.s.ebscohost.com/ehost/pdfviewer/pdfviewer?vid=7&sid=bae776cd-d632-41e6-b7da-fc269f86b-d26%40redis.

14 Alistair Begg, *In the Hand of God: Finding His Care in All Circumstances* (Chicago: Moody Press, 1999), 102-104.

15 Stott, 303.

Chapter 2

16 Strobel, 28.

17 Ibid., 25

18 The Confession of Faith in *The Standards of the Associate Reformed Presbyterian Church* (General Synod of the Associate Reformed Presbyterian Church, 2001), 3:1; 5:1.

19 George M. Schwab, "The Book of Job and Counsel in the Whirlwind," *The Journal of Biblical Counseling* 17:1 (Fall 1998): 31. https://web.s.ebscohost.com/ehost/pdfviewer/pdfviewer?vid=4&sid=5ffc0844-e33d-4cd6-a0ff-a2bfe3279ebd%40redis.

20 Zylstra, n.p.

21 Rohr, 13.

22 Hesselgrave, 77-79.

23 Layton Talbert, *Beyond Suffering: Discovering the Message of Job* (Greenville: Bob Jones University Press, 2007), 15-16.

24 J. I. Packer, *Knowing God* (Downers Grove: Inter-Varsity Press, 1993) 98.

25 John H. Walton and Temper Longman III, *How to*

Read Job (Downers Grove: InterVarsity Press, 2015), 38.

26 R. K. Harrison, *Introduction to the Old Testament* (Grand Rapids: William B Eerdmans Publishing Company, 1991), 1002.

27 Francis I. Anderson, *Job* (Leicester, England: Inter-Varsity Press, n.d.), 15-16.

28 Packer, *Knowing God*, 94-97.

29 Ortlund, 253.

30 Talbert, 22.

31 The Confession of Faith, 3:1; 5:1.

32 Ibid., 13-14, 35.

33 Walter C. Kaiser Jr., *The Majesty of God in the Midst of Innocent Suffering: The Message of Job* (Geanies House, Ross-shire, Scotland: Christian Focus Publications, Ltd, 2019), 16-17.

34 Walton and Longman, 44.

35 David J. A. Clines, *Job 21-37* WBC 18A (Nashville: Thomas Nelson, 2006), 594.

36 Michael D. Fiorello, "Aspects of Intimacy with God in the Book of Job," *Journal of Spiritual Formation*

& *Soul Care* 4:2 (Fall 2011): 163. https://web.s.ebsco-host.com/ehost/pdfviewer/pdfviewer?vid=7&sid=0e1ef45 2-ae8f-4bdf-b21b-248a363f03db%40redis.

37 Gustavo Gutiérrez, *On Job: God-Talk and the Suffering of the Innocent*, trans. Matthew J. O'Connell (Maryknoll: Orbis Books, 1987), 4.

38 David R. Jackson, "Cosmic Bully or God's Grace? The Book of Job as Māšāl," *The Westminster Theological Journal* 78:1 (Spring 2016): 68. https:// web.s.ebscohost.com/ehost/pdfviewer/pdfviewer?vid=10 &sid=0e1ef452-ae8f-4bdf-b21b-248a363f03db%40redis.

39 Schwab, 31.

40 Fiorello, 157-158.

41 Daniel C. Timmer, "Job, Suffering, and the Gospel," *Puritan Reformed Journal* 9:2 (July 2017): 14. https://web.s.ebscohost.com/ehost/pdfviewer/pdfviewer ?vid=19&sid=0e1ef452-ae8f-4bdf-b21b-248a363f03d-b%40redis.

42 Carson, 124.

43 Walton and Longman, 23.

44 David Lambert, "The Book of Job in Ritual Perspective," *Journal of Biblical Literature* 134:3 (2015):

562. https://web.s.ebscohost.com/ehost/pdfviewer/pd-fviewer?vid=13&sid=0e1ef452-ae8f-4bdf-b21b-248a36 3f03db%40redis.

45 Rohr, 48-53.

46 Walton and Longman, 24, 71, 95.

47 Larry J. Waters, "Elihu's Categories of Suffering from Job 32-37," *Bibliotheca Sacra* 166:664 (Oct-Dec 2009): 407-409.https://web.s.ebscohost.com/ehost/pd-fviewer/pdfviewer?vid=22&sid=0e1ef452-ae8f-4bdf-b21 b-248a363f03db%40redis.

48 Antony F. Campbell, "God and Suffering - 'It Happens' Job's Silent Solution," *American Theological Inquiry* 3:1 (Jan 2010): 154-155. https://web.s.ebscohost. com/ehost/pdfviewer/pdfviewer?vid=4&sid=0e1ef452-ae 8f-4bdf-b21b-248a363f03db%40redis.

49 Bill Thomason, *God on Trial: The Book of Job and Human Suffering* (Collegeville: The Liturgical Press, 1997), 70.

50 Timmer, 17.

51 Waters, 415.

52 Tremper Longman III, *Job*, Baker Commentary on

the Old Testament Wisdom and Psalms (Grand Rapids: Baker Academic, 2016), 332-335.

53 Ortlund, 254.

54 Schwab, 37-39.

55 Walton and Longman, 97.

56 Hesselgrave, 23.

57 Ibid., 50-52.

58 Steven J. Lawson, *Preaching the Psalms: Unlocking the Unsearchable Riches of David's Treasury* (Grand Rapids: EP Books, 2012), 101-107.

59 Timmer, 15-17.

60 Lawson, 104.

61 John MacArthur, Jr. *The Power of Suffering: Strengthening Your Faith in the Refiner's Fire* (Wheaton: Victor Books, 1995), 52-58.

62 Walton and Longman, 105.

63 R. C. Sproul, *1-2 Peter: An Expositional Commentary* (Sanford: Reformation Trust, 2019), 18-20, 67.

64 Ibid., 166.

65 Timmer, 18.

66 Walton and Longman, 159.

67 Jackson, 73.

68 "The Shorter Catechism Q14," 290.

69 Philip Yancey, *Where Is God When It Hurts: A Comfort, Healing Guide for Coping with Hard Times* (Grand Rapids: Zondervan Publishing House, 1990), 61.

70 "The Shorter Catechism Q14" *Westminster Confession of Faith* (Glasgow: Free Presbyterian Publications, 2009), 290.

71 Carson, 42-43.

72 John H. Timmerman, *A Season of Suffering: One Family's Journey Through Depression* (Portland: Multnomah Press, 1987), 162-163.

73 Sinclair B. Ferguson, *Deserted by God?* (Grand Rapids: Baker Books, 1993), 80.

74 Carson, 47.

75 James Dobson, *When God Doesn't Make Sense* (Wheaton: Tyndale House Publishers, 1993), 8-9.

76 M. Elizabeth Lewis Hall, Richard C. Langer,

Jason McMartin, "The Role of Suffering in Human Flourishing: Contributions from Positive Psychology, Theology, and Philosophy," *Journal of Psychology & Theology* 38:2 (Sum 2010): 116. https://web.s.ebsco-host.com/ehost/pdfviewer/pdfviewer?vid=17&sid=bae-776cd-d632-41e6-b7da-fc269f86bd26%40redis.

77 Carson, 72.

78 James Boice, "Special Announcement by Dr. James Boice Concerning His Health Difficulties." accessed March 10, 2020. https://drive.google.com/drive/folders/0BzE206wkLf56UkM0N2tVNXQwRnM.

79 This is a poem entitled "When God Wants to Drill a Man." It is not attributed to any particular author. accessed April 1, 2020, http://domenicmarb.blogspot.com/2017/09/origin-of-poem-when-god-wants-to-drill.html.

80 Easter Liu, "Do You Not Care? A Reflection on Suffering and the Heart of the Cross," *The Journal of Biblical Counseling*, 35,2 (2021): 61-64. https://web.s.eb-scohost.com/ehost/pdfviewer/pdfviewer?vid=4&sid=5dd d07d8-601e-4e73-aaa1-2c1b91bf01bb%40redis.

81   Joni Eareckson Tada and Steven Estes, *When God Weeps, Why Our Suffering Matters to the Almighty*

(Grand Rapids: Zondervan Publishing House, 1997), 53-54.

82 Stott, 165.

83Carson, 191.

84 Derek W. H. Thomas, *Heaven on Earth: What the Bible Teaches about Life to Come* (Ross-shire, Scotland: Christian Focus Publications, Ltd., 2018), 15.

85Nancy Guthrie, *Holding on to Hope: A Pathway Through Suffering to the Heart of God* (Wheaton: Tyndale House Publishers, 2002), 64-65.

86 MacArthur, 36.

87 Yancey, 100.

88Carson, 140.

89Annie Johnson Flint hymn, *He Giveth More Grace* has been a huge part of my understanding of God's work in my life. Her faith and attitude in the midst of her suffering has inspired me. So often I find myself depending on my "hoarded resources" instead of depending on the grace and mercy of my Savior.

90 N. T. Wright, "Christianity Offers No Answers About Coronavirus. It's Not Supposed To," *Time*, March

29, 2020, 1-8.https://time.com/5808495/coronavi-rus-christianity/.

91 William Edgar, "Reflections on COVID-19 From Psalm 80," *Unio cum Christo* 7: (Apr 2021): 127-129. https://content.ebscohost. com/ContentServer.asp?T=P&P=AN&K=AT-LAiREM210530000669&S=R&D=lsdar&Ebsco-Content=dGJyMNLr40Sep7Q4v%2BvlOLCmsE-qep7JSr6y4Ta6WxWXS&ContentCustomer=dG-JyMPGutk21r69JuePfgeyx44Dt6fIA.

92 N. T. Wright, *God and the Pandemic: A Christian Reflection on the Coronavirus and Its Aftermath* (Grand Rapids: Zondervan Reflective, 2020), 64-65.

Chapter 3

93 Stott, 303.

94 John Frame, *Systematic Theology: An Introduction to Christian Belief* (Phillipsburg: P&R Publishing, 2013), 169.

95 J. van Genderen and W. H. Velema, *Concise Reformed Dogmatics*, trans. Gerrit Bilkes and Ed M. van der Maas (Phillipsburg: P&R Publishing, 2008), 256, 308-309.

96 C. S. Lewis, *The Problem of Pain* (New York: Touchstone, 1996), 83.

97 Langberg, 50-59.

98 John M. Frame, *Apologetics to the Glory of God* (Phillipsburg: P&R Publishing, 1994) 193-195.

Chapter 4

99 Packer, *Knowing God*, 202.

100 A. W. Pink, *The Attributes of God* (San Bernardino: Codex Spiritualis Publication, 2015.), 57.

101 A. W. Tozer, *The Attributes of God: A Journey into the Father's Heart*, vol. 2 (Chicago: Wings Spread Publishers, 2007), 159-160.

102 David Powlison, *God's Grace in Your Suffering* (Wheaton: Crossway, 2018), 14.

103 John Murray, *Behind a Frowning Providence* (Carlisle: The Banner of Truth Trust, 2017), 10-21.

104 Sunday Bobai Agang, "Divine Sovereignty: The Challenge of Christians Coping with Suffering in the 21st Century," *Kagoro Journal of Theology* 1,1 (2016): 17-30.

https://web.s.ebscohost.com/ehost/

pdfviewer/pdfviewer?vid=4&sid=99b-
72cc4-526b-4bf9-a194-078a9b5db1ec%40redis.

105 John Piper, "Governor of all," *World*, October 6,
2001, 37. From a copy of the article.

106 The Confession of Faith, 2:1.

107 Derek Rishmawy, "The Beauty of the Impassible God: Or, Is God an Emotional Teenager?" *Mere
Orthodoxy* (January 15, 2014): 5-11, accessed August
28, 2022. https://mereorthodoxy.com/beauty-impassi-
ble-god-god-emotional-teenager/.

108 Barry Cooper, "Impassibility." (December 21,
2021): 1-4, accessed August 30, 2022. https://www.ligo-
nier.org/podcasts/simply-put/impassibility.

109 Amos Winarto Oei, "The Impassible God Who
"Cried."" *Themelios* 41,2 (2016): 3-13. https://www.
thegospelcoalition.org/themelios/article/the-impassible-
god-who-cried/.

110 Stott, 323.

111 Kenneth Cauthen, "The Passion of God: Divine
Suffering in Contemporary Protestant Theology," *Journal
of American Academy Religion* 54,2 (Sum 1986): 381.
A review of book by the same name written by Warren

McWilliams. https://web.s.ebscohost.com/ehost/pdfviewer/pdfviewer?vid=8&sid=9eae12e5-b20c-4696-95e2-80907450a7a2%40redis.

112 Kevin DeYoung, "Divine Impassibility and the Passion of Christ in the Book of Hebrews." *The Westminster Theological Journal* 68,1 (Spr 2006): 42-43. https://web.s.ebscohost.com/ehost/pdfviewer/pdfviewer?vid=3&sid=d59000a9-11af-4ce7-9fa0-36474b8c-277c%40redis. DeYoung quotes from Richard Rice's article, "Biblical Support for a New Perspective" in *The Openness of God: A Biblical Challenge to the Traditional Understanding of God.*

113 Ibid., 43.

114 Rishmawy, 2.

115 Frame, *Systematic Theology: An Introduction to Christian Belief*, 412-418.

116 Oei, 3-13.

117 Rishmawy, 5-11.

118 J. I. Packer, "Immutability and Impassibility." accessed August 22, 2022. https://www.youtube.com/watch?v=UvTlF3FuHDk.

119 Carson, 186-188.

Chapter 5

120 MacArthur, 91-105.

121 Martyn Lloyd-Jones, *The Cross* (Wheaton: Cross-way Books, 1986), 213-215.

122 Peter Kreeft, *Making Sense out of Suffering* (Ann Arbor: Servant Books, 1986), 133- 138.

123 Part of a poem, *A New Leaf*, by Helen Field Fischer. https://www.poetrynook.com/poem/new-leaf.

124 Carson, 191.

125 Carson, 246.

Chapter 6

126 Joni Eareckson Tada and Steven Estes, 232-240.

127 John H. Walton and Tremper Longman III, 132-137.

128 Layton Talbert, 14.

129 Eric Ortlund, 256-257.

130 Packer, Knowing God, 97.

131 Drew Hensley, "The Unique Gift of Grief." accessed July 20, 2020. https://www.keylife.org/articles/

the-unique-gift-of-grief/.

132 Derek Thomas, Calvin's Teaching on Job: Proclaiming the Incomprehensible God (Geanies House, Ross-shire, Scotland: Christian Focus Publications, 2016), 223-225.

133 Murray, 10-21.

134 Tripp, 173-184.

135 Agang, 17-30.

136 Dobson, 102.

Chapter 7

137 Tripp, 189-202.

138 Ibid., 205.

139 Jerry K. Robbins, "A Pastoral Approach to Evil" *Theology Today*, 44,4 (Jan 1988): 491-494. https:// web.p.ebscohost.com/ehost/pdfviewer/pdfviewer?vid=5& sid=5efc4290-476c-4827-b50f-01b2d40397be%40redis.

140 John H. Walton and Tremper Longman III, 132-137. David Giese, "Trusting God When Your Boat is Sinking" *The Journal of Evangelical Homiletics Society*, 16,2 (Sep 2016): 45-46. https://web.p.ebscohost.com/ ehost/pdfviewer/pdfviewer?vid=3&sid=5efc4290-476c-4

827-b50f-01b2d40397be%40redis.

141 Nancy Guthrie, *What Grieving People Wish You Knew* (Wheaton: Crossway, 2016), 69.

142 Joni Eareckson Tada, *Songs of Suffering: 25 Hymns and Devotions for Weary Souls* (Wheaton: Crossway, 2022), 17-19.

Appendix 1

143 Nieuwhof, "5 Reasons You Still Feel Disoriented, Dissatisfied, and Depleted (The Challenge of Crisis Leadership)." 2-11. Accessed July 11, 2022. https://careynieuwhof.com/5-reasons-you-still-feel-disoriented-dissatisfied-and-depleted-the-challenge-of-crisis-leadership/.

144 Pew Research Center, "Most Americans Say Coronavirus Outbreak Has Impacted Their Lives" *Pew Research Center*, (March 30, 2020): 4-8, accessed July 7, 2022. https://www.pewresearch.org/social-trends/2020/03/30/most-americans-say-coronavirus-outbreak-has-impacted-their-lives/.

145 Pew Research Center, "More Americans Than People in Other Advanced Economies Say COVID-19 Has Strengthened Religious Faith" *Pew Research Center*, (January 27, 2021): 3-6, accessed August 10, 2022.

https://www.pewresearch.org/religion/wpcontent/uploads/sites/7/2021/01/01.27.21_covid.religion.report.pdf.

146 Pew Research Center, "Few Americans Blame God or Say Faith Has Been Shaken Amid Pandemic, Other Tragedies" *Pew Research Center*, (November 23, 2021): 1-5, accessed August 12, 2022.https://www.pewresearch.org/religion/2021/11/23/few-americans-blame-god-or-say-faith-has-been-shaken-amid-pandemic-other-tragedies/.

147 Pew Research Center, "Most Americans Who Go to Religious Services Say They Would Trust Their Clergy's Advice on COVID-19 Vaccines" *Pew Research Center*, (October 15, 2021): 4-6, accessed July 7, 2022. https://www.pewresearch.org/religion/2021/10/15/most-americans-who-go-to-religious-services-say-they-would-trust-their-clergys-advice-on-covid-19-vaccines/.

148 M. Elizabeth Lewis Hall, Jason Martin, David Wang, Laura Shannonhouse, Jamie D. Aten, Eric J. Silverman, Lauren A. Decker, The Christian Sanctification of Suffering Scale: Measure Development and Relationship to Well-being" *Mental Health, Religion & Culture*, 24,8 (2021): 797-800. https://web.s.ebscohost.com/ehost/pdfviewer/pdfviewer?vid=13&sid=9812a850-5aba-49d9-af3f-71283c75ff67%40redis.

149 Kenneth T. Wang, Krista J. Cowan, Cynthia B. Eriksson, Matthew Januzik, Moriah R. Conant, "Religious Views of Suffering Profile Groups During COVID-19" *Religions*, 13,5 (May 2022): 1-3. https://web.s.ebscohost.com/ehost/pdfviewer/pdfviewer?vid=15&sid=9812a850-5aba-49d9-af3f-71283c75ff67%40redis.

150 Ibid., 3-7

151 Bryan Goodman, "Faith in a Time of Crisis" *American Psychological Association* (May 11, 2020): 2-3.https://www.apa.org/topics/covid-19/faith-crisis.

152 Rian Venter, "Theology, Philosophy of Biology and Virology: An Interdisciplinary Conversation in the Time of COVID-19" *Verbum et Ecclesia*, 42,2, (2021): 6. https://web.s.ebscohost.com/ehost/pdfviewer/pdfviewer?vid=3&sid=2a4e8d09-7551-47b0-a274-a07e34fc-347b%40redis.

153 Lea M. De Backer, "COVID-19 Lockdown in South Africa: Addition, Christian Spirituality and Mental Health" *Verbum et Ecclesia*, 42,1 (2021): 3. https://web.s.ebscohost.com/ehost/pdfviewer/pdfviewer?vid=6&sid=2a4e8d09-7551-47b0-a274-a07e34fc347b%40redis.

154 Wright, "Christianity Offers No Answers About

Coronavirus. It's Not Supposed To" 2-7.

155 Wright, *God and the Pandemic: A Christian Reflection on the Coronavirus and Its Aftermath*), 64-65.

156 John C. Lennox, *Where is God in a Coronavirus World?* 2nd ed. (United Kingdom: The Good Book Company, 2021), 16-30.

157 Ibid., 60-62.

BIBLIOGRAPHY

The Bible — New International Version (1984).

Agang, Sunday Bobai. "Divine Sovereignty: The Challenge of Christians Coping with Suffering in the 21st Century." *Kagoro Journal of Theology* 1,1 (2016): 17-33. https://web.s.ebscohost.com/ehost/pdfviewer/pdfviewer?vid=4&sid=99b-72cc4-526b-4bf9-a194-078a9b5db1ec%40redis.

Anderson, Francis I. *Job*. Leicester, England: InterVarsity Press, n.d.

Begg, Alistair. *In the Hand of God: Finding His Care in All Circumstances*. Chicago: Moody Press, 1999.

Boice, James. "Special Announcement by Dr. James Boice Concerning His Health Difficulties." Accessed March 10, 2020. https://drive.google.com/drive/folders/0BzE206wkLf56UkM0N2tVNX-QwRnM.

Campbell, Antony F. "God and Suffering - 'It Happens': Job's Silent Solution." *American Theological Inquiry* 3,1 (Jan 2010): 253-263. https://web.s.ebscohost.com/ehost/pdfviewer/pdfviewer?vid=4&sid=0e1ef452-ae8f-4bdf-b21b-248a363f03db%40redis.

Carson, D. A. *How Long O Lord?: Reflections on Suffering and Evil*. Grand Rapids: Baker Books, 1990.

Cauthen, Kenneth. "The Passion of God: Divine Suffering in Contemporary Protestant Theology." *The Journal of the American Academy of Religion* 54,2 (Sum 1986): 380-381. Review of book of same name by Warren McWilliams. https://web.s.ebscohost.com/ehost/pdfviewer/pdfviewer?vid=8&sid=5ddd07d8-601e-4e73-aaa1-2c1b91bf01bb%40redis.

Cline, David J. A. *Job 21-37* WBC 18A. Nashville: Thomas Nelson, 2006.

The Confession of Faith 3:1; 5:1. *The Standards of the Associate Reformed Presbyterian Church*. General Synod of the Associate Reformed Presbyterian Church, 2001.

Cooper, Barry. "Impassibility." (December 21, 2021): 1-4. Accessed August 30, 2022. https://www.ligonier.org/podcasts/simply-put/impassibility.

Davis, Steven, ed. *Encountering Evil: Live Options in Theodicy*, new ed. Louisville: Westminster John Knox Press, 2001.

De Backer, Lea M. "COVID-19 Lockdown in South Africa: Addition, Christian Spirituality and Mental Health" *Verbum et Ecclesia*, 42,1 (2021): 3. https://web.s.ebscohost.com/ehost/pdfviewer/pdfviewer?vid=6&sid=2a4e8d09-7551-47b0-a274-a07e34fc347b%40redis.

DeYoung, Kevin. "Divine Impassibility and the Passion of Christ in the Book of Hebrews." *The Westminster Theological Journal* 68,1 (Spr 2006): 41-50. https://web.s.ebscohost.com/ehost/pdfviewer/pdfviewer?vid=3&sid=-d59000a9-11af-4ce7-9fa0-36474b8c277c%40redis.

Dobson, James. *Holding on to Your Faith Even When God Doesn't Make Sense*. Wheaton: Tyndale House Publishers, 1993.

Edgar, William. "Reflections on COVID-19 From Psalm 80," *Unio cum Christo* 7: (Apr 2021): 127-130. https://content.ebscohost.com/ContentServer.asp?T=P&P=AN&K=AT-LAiREM210530000669&S=R&D=lsdar&Esbco-Content=dGJyMNLr40Sep7Q4v%2BvlOLCmsE-qep7JSr6y4Ta6WxWXS&ContentCustomer=dG-JyMPGutk21r69JuePfgeyx44Dt6fIA.

Ferguson, Sinclair B. *Deserted by God?* Grand Rapids: Baker Books, 1993.

Fiorello, Michael D. "Aspects of Intimacy with God in the Book of Job." *Journal of Spiritual Formation & Soul Care* 4,2 (Fall 2011): 155-184. https://web.s.ebscohost.com/ehost/pdfviewer/pdfviewer?vid=7&sid=0e1ef452-ae8f-4bdf-b21b-24 8a363f03db%40redis.

Fisher, Helen Field. "*A New Leaf.*" https://www.poetrynook.com/poem/new-leaf.

Frame, John M. *Apologetics to the Glory of God*. Phillipsburg: P&R Publishing, 1994.

_____. *Systematic Theology: An Introduction to Christian Belief.* Phillipsburg: P&R Publishing, 2013.

Genderen, J. van and W. H. Velema. *Concise Reformed Dogmatics.* Translated by Gerrit Bilkes and Ed M. van der Maas. Phillipsburg: P&R Publishing, 2008.

Giese, David. "Trusting God When Your Boat is Sinking" *The Journal of the Evangelical Homiletics Society* 16,2 (Spr 2016): 42-46.
https://web.p.ebscohost.com/ehost/pdfviewer/pd-fviewer?vid=3&sid=5efc4290-476c-4827-b50f-01b2d40397be%40redis.

Goodman, Bryan. "Faith in a Time of Crisis" *American Psychological Association* (May 11, 2020): 1-7.
https://www.apa.org/topics/covid-19/faith-crisis.

Gore, R. J. "The Problem of Pain." Accessed February 3, 2020. https://drive.google.com/drive/fold-ers/1OKmsX8R8gmT8QO1cg-expPOwmdjvin1S.

Guthrie, Nancy. *Holding On to Hope: A Pathway through Suffering to the Heart of God.* Wheaton: Tyndale House Publishers, 2002.

_____. *What Grieving People Wish You Knew.* Wheaton: Crossway, 2016.

Gutiérrez, Gustavo. *On Job: God-Talk and Suffering of the Innocent,* trans. Matthew J. O'Connell. Maryknoll: Orbis Books, 1987.

Hall, M. Elizabeth Lewis and Richard C. Langer, Jason McMartin. "The Role of Suffering in Human Flourishing: Contributions from Positive Psychology, Theology, and Philosophy." *Journal of Psychology & Theology* 38,2 (Sum 2010): 111-121. https://web.s.ebscohost.com/ehost/pd-fviewer/pdfviewer?vid=17&sid=bae-776cd-d632-41e6-b7da-fc269f86bd26%40redis.

Hall, M. Elizabeth Lewis, Jason Martin, David Wang, Laura Shannonhouse, Jamie D. Aten, Eric J. Silverman, Lauren A. Decker. "The Christian Sanctification of Suffering Scale: Measure Development and Relationship to Well-being" *Mental Health, Religion & Culture*, 24,8 (2021): 796-813. https://web.s.ebscohost.com/ehost/pdfviewer/pd-fviewer?vid=13&sid=9812a850-5aba-49d9-af3f-71283c75ff67%40redis.

Harrison, R. K. *Introduction to the Old Testament*. Grand Rapids: William B Eerdmans Publishing Company, 1991.

Hensley, Drew. "The Unique Gift of Grief." Accessed on July 20, 2020. https://www.keylife.org/articles/the-unique-gift-of-grief/.

Hesselgrave, Ronald P. *I Know that My Redeemer Lives: Suffering and Redemption in the Book of Job*. Eugene: WIPF & Stock, 2016.

Jackson, David R. "Cosmic Bully or God's Grace? The Book of Job as Māšāl," *The Westminster Theological Journal* 78:1 (Spr 2016): 65-73. https://web.s.ebscohost.com/ehost/pdfviewer/pd-

fviewer?vid=10&sid=0e1ef452-ae8f-4bdf-b21b-2
48a363f03db%40redis.

Kaiser, Jr., Walter C. *The Majesty of God in the Midst of Innocent Suffering: The Message of Job.* Geanies House, Ross-shire, Scotland: Christian Focus Publications, Ltd. 2019.

Kreeft, Peter. *Making Sense Out of Suffering.* Ann Arbor: Servant Books, 1986.

Lambert, David. "The Book of Job in Ritual Perspective." *Journal of Biblical Literature* 134, 3 (2015): 557-575.
https://web.s.ebscohost.com/ehost/pdfviewer/pd-fviewer?vid=13&sid=0e1ef452-ae8f-4bdf-b21b-2
48a363f03db%40redis.

Langberg, Diane. *Suffering and the Heart of God: How Trauma Destroys and Christ Restores.* Greensboro: New Growth Press, 2015.

Lawson, Steven J. *Preaching the Psalms: Unlocking the Unsearchable Riches of David's Treasury.* Grand Rapids: EP Books, 2012.

Lennox, John C. *Where is God in a Coronavirus World?* 2nd ed. United Kingdom: The Good Book Company, 2021.

Lewis, C. S. *A Grief Observed.* New York: HarperCollins Publishers, 1996.

_____. *The Problem of Pain.* New York: Touchstone, 1996.

Liu, Esther. "Do You Not Care? A Reflection on Suffering and the Heart of Christ." *The Journal of Biblical Counseling* 35,2 (2021): 60-65. https://web.s.ebscohost.com/ehost/pdfviewer/pdfviewer?vid=4&sid=5ddd07d8-601e-4e73-aaa1-2c1b91bf01bb%40redis.

Lloyd-Jones, Martyn. *The Cross*. Wheaton: Crossway Books, 1986.

Longman III, Tremper. *Job*, Baker Commentary on the Old Testament Wisdom and Psalms. Grand Rapids: Baker Academic, 2016.

MacArthur, John. *The Power of Suffering.* Wheaton: Victor Books, 1995.

Murray, John. *Behind a Frowning Providence*. Carlisle: The Banner of Truth Trust, 2017.

Nieuwhof, Carey, "5 Reasons You Still Feel Disoriented, Dissatisfied, and Depleted (The Challenge of Crisis Leadership)." 1-15. Accessed July 11, 2022. https://careynieuwhof.com/5-reasons-you-still-feel-disoriented-dissatisfied-and-depleted-the-challenge-of-crisis-leadership/.

Oei, Amos Winarto. "The Impassible God Who "Cried."" *Themelios* 41,2 (2016): 1-16. https://www.thegospelcoalition.org/themelios/article/the-impassible-god-who-cried/.

Ortlund, Eric. "Five Truths for Sufferers from the Book of Job." *Themelios* 40,2 (Aug 2015): 253-262. https://web.s.ebscohost.com/ehost/pd-

fviewer/pdfviewer?vid=7&sid=bae-
776cd-d632-41e6-b7da-fc269f86bd26%40redis.

Packer, J. I. "Immutability and Impassibility." Accessed
August 22, 2022.   https://www.youtube.com/
watch?v=UvTlF3FuHDk.

_____. *Knowing God*. Downers Grove: InterVarsity
Press, 1993.

Pew Research Center. "Few Americans Blame God or
Say Faith Has Been Shaken Amid Pandemic, Other Tragedies" *Pew Research Center* (November
23, 2021): 1-12. Accessed August 12, 2022.
https://www.pewresearch.org/religion/2021/11/23/
few-americans-blame-god-or-say-faith-has-been-
shaken-amid-pandemic-other-tragedies/.

_____. "More Americans Than People in Other Ad-
vanced Economies Say COVID-19 Has Strengthened Religious Faith" *Pew Research Center* (January 27, 2021): 1-18. Accessed August 10, 2022.
https://www.pewresearch.org/religion/wp-content/
uploads/sites/7/2021/01/01.27.21_covid.religion.
report.pdf.

_____. "Most Americans Say Coronavirus Outbreak
Has Impacted Their Lives" *Pew Research Center*
(March 30, 2020): 1-25. Accessed July 7, 2022.
https://www.pewresearch.org/so-
cial-trends/2020/03/30/most-americans-say-coro-
navirus-outbreak-has-impacted-their-lives/.

_____. "Most Americans Who Go to Religious
Services Say They Would Trust Their Clergy's

Advice on COVID-19 Vaccines" *Pew Research Center* (October 15, 2021): 1-28. Accessed July 7, 2022. https://www.pewresearch.org/religion/2021/10/15/most-americans-who-go-to-religious-services-say-they-would-trust-their-clergys-advice-on-covid-19-vaccines/.

Pink, A.W. *The Attributes of God.* San Bernardino: Codex Spiritualis Publications 2015.

Piper, John. "Governor of all," *Time*, October 6, 2001.

Powlison, David. *God's Grace in Your Suffering.* Wheaton: Crossway, 2018.

Rishmawy, Derek. "The Beauty of the Impassible God: Or, Is God and Emotional Teenager?" *Mere Orthodoxy* (January 15, 2014): 1-13. Accessed August 28, 2022. https://mereorthodoxy.com/beauty-impassible-god-god-emotional-teenager/.

Robbins, Jerry K. "A Pastoral Approach to Evil" *Theology Today* 44,4 (Jan 1988): 488-496. https://web.p.ebscohost.com/ehost/pdfviewer/pdfviewer?vid=5&sid=5efc4290-476c-4827-b50f-01b2d40397be%40redis.

Rohr, Richard. *Job and the Mystery of Suffering: Spiritual Reflection.* New York: The Crossroad Publishing Company, 2019.

Schwab, George M. "The Book of Job and the Counsel in the Whirlwind." *The Journal of Biblical Counsel-*

ing 17,1 (Fall 1998): 31-43. https://web.s.ebsco-host.com/ehost/pdfviewer/pdfviewer?vid=4&sid=5ffc0844-e33d-4cd6-a0ff-a2bfe3279ebd%40redis.

Sproul, R. C. *1-2 Peter: An Expositional Commentary.* Sanford: Reformation Trust, 2019.

Stott, John R., *The Cross of Christ*, 20th anniversary ed. Downers Grove: InterVarsity Press, 2006.

Strobel, Lee. *The Case for Faith: A Journalist Investigates the Toughest Questions to Christianity.* Grand Rapids: Zondervan, 2000.

Tada, Joni Eareckson. *Songs of Suffering: 25 Hymns and Devotions for Weary Souls.* Wheaton: Crossway, 2022.

Tada, Joni Eareckson and Steven Estes. *When God Weeps, Why Our Suffering Matters to the Almighty.* Grand Rapids: Zondervan, 1997.

Talbert, Layton. *Beyond Suffering: Discovering the Message of Job.* Greenville: Bob Jones University Press, 2007.

Thomas, Derek. *Calvin's Teaching on Job: Proclaiming the Incomprehensible God.* Geanies House, Ross-shire, Scotland: Christian Focus Publications, 2016.

_____. *Heaven on Earth: What the Bible Teaches about the Heart of God.* Ross-shire, Scotland: Christian Focus Publications, Ltd., 2018.

Thomason, Bill. *God on Trial: The Book of Job and Human Suffering.* Collegeville: The Liturgical Press, 1997.

Timmer, Daniel C. "Job, Suffering, and the Gospel." *Puritan Reformed Journal* 9,2 (July 2017): 5-20. https://web.s.ebscohost.com/ehost/pdfviewer/pdfviewer?vid=19&sid=0e1ef452-ae8f-4bdf-b21b-248a363f03db%40redis.

Timmerman, John H. *A Season of Suffering: One Family's Journey Through Depression.* Portland: Multnomah Press, 1987.

Tozer, A.W. *The Attributes of God,* vol 2. Chicago: Wing Spread Publishers, 2007.

Tripp, Paul David. *Suffering: Gospel Hope When Life Doesn't Make Sense.* Wheaton: Crossway, 2018.

"The Shorter Catechism Q14" *Westminster Confession of Faith,* Glasgow, Scotland: Free Presbyterian Publications, 2009.

Unknown Author. "When God Wants to Drill A Man." Accessed April 1, 2020. https://domenicmarb.blogspot.com/2017/09/origin-of-poem-when-god-wants-to-drill.html.

Venter, Rian. "Theology, Philosophy of Biology and Virology: An Interdisciplinary Conversation in the Time of COVID-19" *Verbum et Ecclesia,* 42,2, (2021): 6. https://web.s.ebscohost.com/ehost/pdfviewer/pdfviewer?vid=3&sid=2a4e8d09-7551-47b0-a274-a07e34fc347b%40redis.

Walton, John H and Temper Longman III. *How to Read Job*. Downers Grove: InterVarsity Press, 2015.

Wang, Kenneth T., Krista J. Cowan, Cynthia B. Eriksson, Matthew Januzik, Moriah R. Conant. "Religious Views of Suffering Profile Groups During COVID-19" *Religions*, 13,5 (May 2022): 1-3. https://web.s.ebscohost.com/ehost/pdfviewer/pdfviewer?vid=15&sid=9812a850-5aba-49d9-af3f-71283c75ff67%40redis.

Waters, Larry J. "Elihu's Categories of Suffering from Job." *Bibliotheca Sacra* 116,664 (Oct-Dec 2009): 405-420. https://web.s.ebscohost.com/ehost/pdfviewer/pdfviewer?vid=22&sid=0e1ef452-ae8f-4bdf-b21b-248a363f03db%40redis.

Wiesel, Elie. *Night*. New York: Hill and Wang, 2006.

White, James Emery. *Christianity for People Who Aren't Christians: Uncommon Answers to Common Questions*. Grand Rapids: Baker Books, 2019.

Wright, N. T. "Christianity Offers No Answers About Coronavirus. It's Not Supposed To," *Time,* March 29, 2020. https://time.com/5808495/coronavirus-christianity/.

_____. *God and the Pandemic: A Christian Reflection on the Coronavirus and Its Aftermath*. Grand Rapids: Zondervan Reflective, 2020.

Yancey, Philip. *Where Is God When It Hurts: A Comfort, Healing Guide for Coping with Hard Times*. Grand Rapids: Zondervan, 1990.

Zylstra, Sarah Eekhoff. "How Chinese Pastors Developed Their Theology for Suffering." *The Gospel Coalition* January 2020. Accessed on June 14, 2020. https://www.thegospelcoalition.org/article/how-chinese-pastors-developed-their-theology-for-suffering/.

Scripture Index

Revelation

About the Author

William S. (Bill) Cain, MDiv, DMin, is pastor of Louisville Associate Reformed Presbyterian Church, where he has served for over ten years. Before entering the full-time pastorate, he was president of Chelsea House, Inc., a decorative furniture and accessories manufacturer. He earned a Bachelor of Science in Business Administration from UNC, Chapel Hill, and his Master of Divinity and Doctor of Ministry degrees from Erskine Theological Seminary in Due West, SC.

Bill has taught across the country and worldwide on various Christian topics, often specializing in the History of the English Bible. He has studied suffering for over twenty years after he was first diagnosed with cancer in 2001. Realizing his own theodicy was insufficient for his life, he began an in-depth look into the Bible for the necessary bedrock truths Christians must have before the inevitable waves of pain and suffering come. The foundation stones of a proper understanding of suffering are critical for the Christian to survive and even thrive in chaotic times. This book is a result of his many years of pastoral work as a chaplain to various first responders and as a shepherd of his congregations.

Bill and his wife, Monica, have made their home in Georgia. They are proud parents to three grown children and doting grandparents to three grandchildren, who bring them immense joy and fulfillment.

Printed in the USA
CPSIA information can be obtained
at www.ICGtesting.com
CBHW050915210724
11863CB00007B/106